Astrology

Astrology

THE STARS AND HUMAN LIFE: A MODERN GUIDE

CHRISTOPHER McINTOSH

MACDONALD UNIT 75

SBN 356 03467 4

© Christopher McIntosh, 1970

First published in 1970 by
Macdonald Unit 75
St Giles House, 49 Poland Street, London W.1.

Made and printed in Great Britain by
Hazell Watson & Viney Ltd, Aylesbury, Bucks

Contents

I

Introduction to Astrology

> One may know everything about astrology and make a mess of one's life. Yet the connection between astrology and the art of living is there, and for me it provides the clue to the survival of a science which has long been termed a pseudo-science. What, I ask, can be more important than the knowledge of how to live one's life on earth?
>
> Henry Miller, Foreword to *Henry Miller: His World of Urania*

WHAT kind of person are you? Most people, at some stage in their lives, ask themselves this question; and most people, when they try to put the answer into words, think in terms of categories: introvert, extrovert; emotional, unemotional; conventional, unconventional; thinker, doer. It is natural for people to think in terms of types, and the chances are that, if you have ever thought about yourself, you would be able to say what type of character you are. It is reassuring to know, or to imagine, that one fits into a particular category; and those who are uncertain of their type are often grateful to be told that they fit into this or that pigeon-hole. And this is part of the reason why astrology appeals to so many people.

Pick up any newspaper and glance at the horoscope column, and you will see that astrology divides the human race into twelve great groups, placing each person under a sign of the zodiac according to the month in which he was born. The astrologer believes that each of these groups has its own distinct characteristics. If you were born under Aries he will tell you that you are bold, energetic, and assertive; if under Taurus then you are possessive, steadfast, and conservative; if you are Geminian you are labelled as lively, versatile, and talkative; if you are a Cancerian you are intuitive, emotional, and domestic. And so it goes on: Leonians are proud, cheerful, magnanimous; Virgoans, modest, practical, hard-working; Librans, pleasant, companionable, tactful; Scorpios, intense, passionate, secretive; Sagittarians, active, restless, adventurous; Capricornians, practical, ambitious, cautious; Aquarians, independent, unconventional, inquisitive; and Pisceans, emotional, intuitive, artistic.

You may think that the description of your own sign is completely different from your own idea of yourself. But if you tackled an astrologer on the subject he might say something like this: 'No, you are not a typical Libra, but then your ascendant is in Scorpio, and you have four planets in Gemini in the tenth house.' In other words, there is a lot more to astrology than the signs of the zodiac.

You would probably not have picked this book up if you were a complete sceptic about astrology. But even if you are, you may agree with the French writer on astrology, Bouché-Leclerq, who said that 'it is not a waste of one's time to study how other people have wasted theirs'. In fact, for the sociologist or anthropologist astrology poses a rather intriguing problem in the study of human belief.

People who scoff at astrology often refer to it as a pseudoscience. And one of the strange things about astrology is that it has never been able to make up its mind whether it is a science or a kind of religion. The result has been that astrology has developed a split personality. Ever since Copernicus, in the 16th century, upset the old astrological picture of the heavens and initiated the era of modern astronomy, astrologers have tended to divide themselves into two camps. On the one hand you have those who would like to see astrology brought back into the scientific fold. They are constantly trying to explain planetary influences in terms of radiations, vibrations, magnetic fields, and so on, and are prepared to scrap the traditional system in favour of something more scientific. On the other hand there are those who say that astrology is not a scientific theory but a symbolic way of looking at the universe, and that the astrological symbols are powerful entities in their own right which have no need to be supported by any scientific proof. For them it is enough that astrology works – why it works is not their concern. Later on I shall be taking a closer look at both these points of view.

In this book I have tried to avoid propaganda – for or against astrology. Nevertheless I would not have written it if I thought that astrology was a complete waste of time. Aleister Crowley once said that there was a fraction of one per cent truth in astrology. I agree with him, but in my opinion that fraction is very valuable.

My first contact with astrology was, like most people's, through the horoscope columns in the newspapers. For years I knew nothing more about it than the name of my zodiacal sign. Then one day a student friend told me that he had been studying astrology and had found that there was a great deal of truth in it. I did not know what to make of this. Until then I had regarded astrology as a vulgar superstition. But I had enough respect for the friend concerned to read some of the books that he recommended to me. The first thing I learned was that astrology was an infinitely complex subject involving a totally new and bewildering vocabulary. Intrigued, I persevered with the subject and in due course was able to cast my own horoscope, which seemed to give a remarkably true assessment of my character. I cast other horoscopes. Sometimes I was able to give a startlingly accurate diagnosis of a person, at other times my conclusions were wildly wrong. But I came to realise that the symbolism of astrology had a strange kind of beauty and inner consistency. It seemed that merely by learning and applying the language of astrology one could see things about people that one could not see if one were using ordinary language. The novelist, Henry Miller, put it this way: 'To look at man's universe with the eyes of an astrologer demands more than the exercise of logic and reason. It requires the vision and imagination of the poet, for whom language has to be created anew. The language of the astrologer is entirely one of symbols – and their meaning is inexhaustible.' Those words come from the foreword to a book called *Henry Miller: His World of Urania*, by the American astrologer Sydney Omarr.

The symbols of astrology are now becoming almost as familiar to people as the symbols of Christianity. The psychologist Carl Jung, who was deeply interested in astrology, would say that these symbols were becoming part of our collective unconscious. One test of how deeply a symbol has sunk into our thinking is whether it is used as a swear word. When you swear you use the most powerful symbols at your disposal, which at the moment are predominantly Christian: 'good God', 'for Christ's sake', and so on. But soon we may hear people saying: 'By Gemini', or 'What the Moon do you think you're doing?' When that happens we will know that astrology has really sunk in.

As I have said, there is a great deal more to astrology than the stuff that is printed in the newspapers. I hope that this brief outline of the subject will give the reader an idea of what it is all about, as well as a glimpse at some of the interesting and unusual ways in which astrology has been used.

2

The Bricks and Mortar of Astrology

> We and the cosmos are one. The cosmos is a vast
> living body of which we are still parts.
>
> D. H. Lawrence, *Apocalypse*

THE three key elements in a horoscope are the signs of the
zodiac, the planets, and the houses. Most readers of newspaper horoscopes are familiar only with the signs. But the
signs by themselves are passive vehicles without any independent power to influence human beings; it is only when
the active forces of the planets vibrate through them that
they spring to life. It is as though the signs were different
types of radio transmitter obeying the varying signals sent
out by the planets. Or, to use another analogy, the planets
are actors on a revolving stage, creating different moods in
the audience as the scenic background shifts.

The stage on which the planets play their parts is a great
belt of stars stretching around the earth. It is 8° wide and
360° in circumference. This belt follows the path – called
the ecliptic – that the Sun appears to trace annually
around the earth. And here it is important to mention that
for the astrologer the earth, and not the Sun, is the centre
of our planetary system. This is not as absurd as it sounds,
for what matters in astrology is the relative positions of
the heavenly bodies *vis-à-vis* the earth at any particular
time. If the earth is for us the focal point of the planetary
forces then it makes perfectly good sense to imagine the
other bodies as revolving around it. The ecliptic, then, is

the Sun's annual path around the earth; or, to be more detailed, if every day at noon you were to mark the point where the Sun's rays struck the earth at a perpendicular and then joined the points together you would trace the line known as the ecliptic.

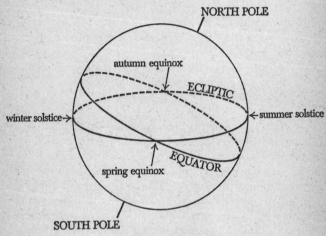

Figure 1

Figure 1 shows that the ecliptic is at a slight angle to the equator. It is this angle that causes the seasons to change. If you live in the northern hemisphere then the height of summer is the point where the ecliptic is farthest from the equator on the northern side. The sun reaches this point at the summer solstice. Similarly, in the depths of winter the Sun is way down at the winter solstice. The opposite of course applies to the southern hemisphere. The solstices lie on the latitudes known as the tropics of Cancer and Capricorn, because the dates on which they occur coincide with the Sun's position in those signs. The term 'tropic' comes from a Greek word meaning 'turning point'. The points where the ecliptic crosses the equator mark the beginning of spring and autumn. These are known as the equinoxes.

Now, to return to the belt of stars we call the zodiac: if you project the ecliptic into the sky and widen it to 8° you get a strip of constellations through which the Sun revolves, rising in a different one every month (see Figure 2). The Babylonians, who invented the zodiac, divided it into twelve parts, because there were twelve lunar months approximately in the solar year. Each group of stars was

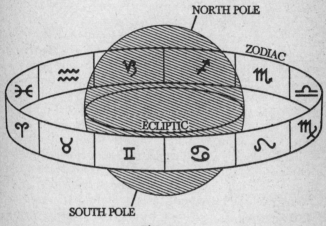

Figure 2

given a name deriving from mythology. I shall talk about these later.

At this point it is important to mention what is known as the precession of the equinoxes. This means that the annual revolution of the Sun through the constellations is not quite constant. Each spring the position of the rising Sun in the zodiac has shifted infinitesimally, so that over a period of two thousand years it shifts through an entire sign, and over 25,920 years it shifts right around the zodiac. Traditionally the first sign of the zodiac is Aries, because the Sun rose in Aries at the spring equinox. But since then the equinox has moved into Pisces and is now entering Aquarius. Some astrologers attach great importance to this movement; hence the widespread obsession with the so-called 'Age of Aquarius' which is believed to be dawning.

Because of the precession of the equinoxes, the signs of the zodiac, as used by traditional astrologers, no longer coincide with the constellations whose names they bear. For example, an astrologer says that at the spring equinox the Sun rises in Aries whereas an astronomer would say that it rises in Pisces. The astrologer is referring to a purely symbolic constellation tied to the time of year; the astronomer is referring to the actual group of stars.

So there are really two zodiacs. First there is the 'tropical' zodiac whose co-ordinates are the 'turning points' of the solar year, the solstices and the equinoxes; this is the one that most traditional astrologers use. Secondly there is the 'sidereal' zodiac which follows the actual positions of the stars in the sky. The name derives from the Latin word *sidus*, meaning a star. The existence of these two zodiacs raises a great dilemma for the astrologer who is anxious to put his system on a scientific basis. I shall talk more about this controversy in a later chapter.

So far I have talked only about the importance of the signs and planets; but there is also the third important element which I mentioned – the houses. To understand the meaning of this term it is necessary once again to grasp a few simple astronomical facts.

The houses, like the signs of the zodiac, are twelve in number; but instead of being divisions of the sky they are divisions of the earth's surface projected into the sky – hence the term 'mundane' which refers to all matters relating to the house. The concept of the houses came into being because the early astrologers were struck with the idea that the constellation that was in the sky over the eastern horizon at the time of birth (known as the ascendant, or rising sign) must be an important factor in an individual horoscope. By the same reasoning, importance must also be attached to the sign on the meridian (mid-heaven, *medium coeli* or MC), the sign on the western horizon (descendant), and the sign immediately below the meridian (lowest heaven *imum coeli* or IC). The areas between these four points were then divided into three sections each, making a total of twelve.

Because the earth makes one complete revolution in twenty-four hours it follows that the ascendant takes roughly two hours to pass through each sign. Hence, if the houses are to be included in a horoscope, it is necessary to know the exact time of day of the subject's birth.

This is, of course, an oversimplification. What I have said holds good only for points near the equator. In northern and southern latitudes some signs remain below the horizon much longer than others, depending on the time of year. Hence astrologers have attempted to find a system of house division that takes these differences into account. The most widely used today is the Placidean system, named after its inventor, Placidus de Titis (1603–1668), a Benedictine monk who taught mathematics at the University of Padua.

The other main system, which is growing in popularity, is the equal house system. This takes no account of the discrepancies I have mentioned, but it has the advantage of being very neat and easy to handle. Since it seems to work just as well as the Placidean system it is the one I have adopted in this book. But before we get down to the technicalities of calculating a horoscope we have to gain a more detailed knowledge of our basic tools, the planets, signs, and houses.

3

The Planets

So may we read, and little find them cold:
Not frosty lamps illumining dead space,
Not distant aliens, not senseless Powers.
The fire is in them whereof we are born;
The music of their motion may be ours.

George Meredith, *Meditation under Stars*

FROM very early times man has been aware of the differences between the stars and the planets. The Babylonians called the planets 'erring stars' and invested them with characters of their own. This was done partly by observation of their natural characteristics and partly by determining what effects they caused on earth. The Babylonian astrologer-priests, from their towers, or *ziggurats*, observed the incidence of floods, earthquakes, wars, and other events accompanying the prominence of each heavenly body. Recordings of this nature, made over a long period, formed the basis of astrology on which other nations were to build. The Greeks and Romans both made their contributions, and the sum total is what has been passed down to us today.

The connections of the planets with various elements in mythology may appear haphazard and arbitrary. But myths are not just fairy tales: they have a special kind of truth. And wherever a planet was connected with a particular mythological figure it was because both the planet and the myth expressed the same truth. The following is a short *Who's Who* of the planets.

☿

Mercury

The Babylonians identified this planet with their god Nabu, son of Marduk. Nabu was the god of intellectual activity. He was also the scribe of the gods and was credited with the invention of writing. Hence he presided over literature.

When astrology passed to the Greeks the planet came to be identified with Hermes, the god of travellers, commerce, and profit. Since buying and selling require a persuasive tongue, Hermes was also the god of eloquence.

As with all the other planets, it is the Roman name that has stuck. The Roman god, Mercury, had much the same characteristics as Hermes. Most people know him through pictures and sculpture. He is the swift, agile fellow with wings on his feet, carrying a rod entwined with snakes. He is a friendly, but mischievous character.

The influence of any planet can, of course, take either a beneficial or an adverse form, depending on whether the planet is well or badly placed in a horoscope. Mercury, when well placed, gives the following characteristics, according to the 17th-century astrologer William Lilly, in his book *Christian Astrology*.

Being well dignified, he represents a man of subtill and politick braine, intellect, and cogitation; an excellent disputant or Logician, arguing with learning and discretion, and using much eloquence in his speech, a searcher into all kinds of Mysteries and Learning, sharp and witty, learning almost anything without a Teacher . . . if he turn Merchant no man exceeds him in way of Trade or invention of new ways whereby to obtain wealth.

When badly placed, Mercury represents 'A troublesome wit, a kinde of Phrenetick man, his tongue and Pen against every man, wholly bent to foole his estate and time in prating and trying his conclusions to no purpose; a great lyar, boaster, pratler, busybody, false, a tale-carrier, given to wicked Arts, as Necromancy, and such like ungodly knowledges.'

To sum up, the main characteristics of Mercury are:

1. Extreme changeability. Ptolemy, the 2nd-century Alexandrian writer on astronomy and astrology, said that Mercury was 'quick to change from one form to another'. This was because Mercury was thought to be particularly sensitive to the influences of the other planets, like the good messenger he was. According to Ptolemy he could not only change from hot to cold or dry to moist, but he could also change sex. It is from this fickle quality that our word 'mercurial' comes.

2. Intelligence. Mercury gives a quick wit and a versatile mind.

3. Eloquence. The mercurial person is extremely fond of talking and is often a skilful raconteur.

4. Artistic ability.

5. Connection with journeys and messages.

♀

Venus

This planet was personified in Babylonia by Ishtar, goddess of the morning and evening. In some areas of Mesopotamia, Venus was worshipped as the goddess of battles and portrayed as a belligerent, warlike personality. But at Erech, centre of the Ishtar cult, she was seen as the goddess of love and sensuality. It was she who was responsible for arousing erotic desire in earthly creatures, and as soon as she withdrew her influence dire consequences followed, as an old Babylonian text describes:

> The bull refuses to cover the cow, the ass no longer
> approaches the she-ass,
> In the street the man no longer approaches the
> maid-servant.

Ishtar's holy city, Erech, was known as the 'town of sacred courtesans' because of the sanctified prostitution surrounding her cult. Although Ishtar was often cruel and vindictive, she was also capable of acts of generosity and kindness towards mortals.

The same characteristics were associated with the Greek goddess Aphrodite and her Roman counterpart, Venus.

Here is what Ptolemy said about the planet: 'When Venus rules alone in a position of glory she renders the mind benignant, good, voluptuous, copious in wit, pure, gay, fond of dancing, abhorring wickedness . . . but, if contrarily posited, she renders the mind dull, amorous, effeminate, timorous, indiscriminating, sordid, faulty, obscure and ignominious.'

The qualities of eroticism, kindness, and warmth of emotion are now considered to be the outstanding characteristics of Venus. The symbol of the planet is used to denote the female sex.

♂

Mars

Possibly because of its red colour, Mars was associated with the fiery, warlike Babylonian god, Nergal. Under the Greeks the planet came to be connected with their war god, Ares. In Homer's *Iliad*, Zeus says to his son Ares: 'Of all the gods who live in Olympus thou art the most odious to me; for thou enjoyest nothing but strife, war and battles. Thou hast the obstinate and unmanageable disposition of thy mother, Hera, whom I can scarcely control with my words.'

This description exactly sums up the character of the planet Mars in astrological tradition. The god from whom the planet takes its name was the Roman equivalent of Ares. The warlike Romans tended to regard him with greater reverence than the Greeks had done.

Here is Lilly's description of Mars. When well placed, he is 'In feats of Warre and Courage invincible, scorning any should exceed him, subject to no Reason, Bold, Confident, immovable, Contentious, challenging all honour to themselves, Valiant, lovers of Warre.'

When badly placed, 'Then he is a pratler without modesty or honesty, a lover of Slaughter and Quarrels, Murder, Theevery, a promoter of Sedition, Frayes and Commotions, an Highway-Theefe, as wavering as the Wind, a Traytor of turbulent Spirit, Perjured, Obscene, Rash, Inhumane . . . Unthankful, Trecherous.'

Our word 'martial' sums up the qualities of the planet. Traditionally Mars was regarded as a planet of evil influence, but today it is recognised that the thrusting aggressiveness imparted by the planet can be good if it is expressed in the right ways Because of the physical vigour of Mars, it is often prominent in the horoscopes of athletes. The planet is also associated with sexual drive, and the symbol is used today to denote the male sex.

♃

Jupiter

This planet was identified by the Babylonians with their god Marduk, who replaced his father Ea as the chief of the gods and was thought of as a wise, benevolent ruler. His Greek equivalent was Zeus, again the king of the gods and a firm, but wise and compassionate ruler. The Roman god after whom the planet is named had a similar position. He was the guardian of the Roman state and symbolised the virtues of justice, good faith and honour.

Lilly described the Jupiterian character as follows. When well placed: 'Then he is Magnanimous, Faithful, Bashfull, Aspiring in an honourable way at high matters, in all his actions a Lover of faire Dealing, desiring to benefit all men, doing Glorious things, Honourable and Religious, of sweet and affable Conversation, wonderfully indulgent to his Wife and Children, reverencing Aged men, a great Reliever of the Poore, full of Charity and Godlinesse, Liberal, hating all Sordid actions, Just, Wise, Prudent, Thankfull, Vertuous.'

When badly placed: 'Then he wastes his Patrimony, suffers every one to cozen him, is Hypocritically Religious, Tenacious, and stiff in maintaining false tenets in Religion; he is Ignorant, Carelesse, nothing delightful in the love of his Friends; of a grosse, dull Capacity, Schismatical, abasing himself in all Companies, crouching and stooping where no necessity is.'

The main characteristics imparted by the planet are:

1. Cheerfulness. Our word 'jovial' is derived from the Latin name for the planet.

2. Wisdom. Jupiter stands for intellect, but of a deeper, more searching kind than shown by the cleverness of Mercury.

3. Religiosity. A prominent Jupiter in a horoscope indicates the possibility of the subject becoming a priest or minister. Recent statistical investigations have born this out to some extent.

♄

Saturn

The first god to be identified with Saturn was the Babylonian god Ninib, or Ninurta. Like Nergal, he was a warlike god. He was the 'strong one who destroys the wicked and the enemy'. Because of his belligerent character he was rather unpopular. The Greek Cronos, with whom the planet was also identified, was an even less likeable character. First he castrated his father, Uranus, and later devoured his own children. The Roman god, Saturn, was more benevolent, governing agriculture and fruitfulness, but it is the evil qualities of the planet that seem to have been retained. Most of the early astrological writers agree in regarding Saturn as a pretty grim sort of character. Ptolemy says: 'Where the world sinks at the foundation of heaven and lost in midnight beholds above it the opposed sky – that is the region where Saturn exercises his strength. Of old was he himself cast down from the empire of heaven and the seat of the gods. . . . A dread title belongs to his realm: *Daemonium* the Greek hath it: and the name betokens clearly the power that dwells here.'

But since Ptolemy's day astrologers have come to take a brighter view of Saturn. The 18th-century astrologer, Ebenezer Sibly, says: 'If this planet is well dignified at the time of birth, the native will be of an acute and penetrating imagination; in his conduct, austere; in words, reserved; in speaking and giving, very spare, in labour, patient; in arguing or disputing, grave; in obtaining the goods of this life, studious and solicitous; in his attachments, either to wife or friend, constant and unequivocal; in prejudice or resentment, rigid and inexorable. But, if this planet be ill dignified at the time of birth, the native will be naturally sordid, envious, covetous, mistrustful, cowardly, sluggish, outwardly dissembling, false, stubborn, malicious, and perpetually dissatisfied with himself and with all about him.'

This more or less coincides with the modern view of Saturn. His less likeable qualities are humourlessness, inhibition and emotional coldness. His good ones are courage, endurance, discipline, practicality and patience.

♅

Uranus

We now come to the three 'new' planets, the first of which was discovered in 1781 by Sir William Herschel. It was originally called after its discoverer, though later it came to be known as Uranus. Astrologers have attributed to

Uranus the qualities of sudden awakening and violent change. Its influence is thought to be disruptive, though not necessarily in a bad sense. It is also thought to be connected with scientific discovery. The symbol is rather like a television aerial, and television happens to be a particularly Uranian invention. Margaret Hone, in her *Modern Text Book of Astrology*, says: 'A key to the understanding of the ability to make and suffer changes, to act unconventionally, often crudely, to act under a flash of intuition rather than by slow reasoning, to incline to all that has to do with modern invention, especially that which uses "rays" or "waves", will be given by the placing of Uranus in sign and house, and by its strength in the chart.'

Ψ

Neptune

This planet was discovered in 1848. Astrologers regard it as an elusive and intangible force. 'Hidden' is the key word for Neptune. It has to do with everything that operates behind the scenes, vicariously, or in disguise. It tends also to represent spiritual and non-material energies. The modern astrologer, Charles E. O. Carter, says in his book, *The Principles of Astrology*, that Neptune 'commonly produces extreme sensitiveness, physical and emotional, and is not only prominent in the nativities of musicians, but also of mediumistic persons'.

♇

Pluto

Discovered in 1930, Pluto has had very little time to be absorbed into the astrological tradition, and there seems to be a certain amount of disagreement about what its effects are. But the general view is that Pluto represents resurgence of the past, release of dormant forces, the sudden eruption of suppressed energies. To quote Margaret Hone again: 'From the time of its discovery, much has gone on which is eruptive. That which was in the dark or bound or enclosed is violently ejected or vice versa. One instance is the development of the atom bomb.'

⊙

Sun

Strictly speaking, of course, the Sun and Moon are not planets, but in the geocentric system used by the astrologers they are considered as such. Thus the 'seven planets' of traditional astrology include the Sun and Moon.

In Babylonia the Sun-god was Shamash, who every day drove his magnificent chariot across the sky from east to west. As the banisher of night and the conqueror of winter, he was characterised by qualities of vigour and courage. He was also the god of justice.

Helios, the Greek counterpart of Shamash, was very similar. He, too, had a chariot which he rode across the sky; and he, too, discovered the crimes of the wicked. But, strange as it may seem, he was a comparatively minor deity in Greece, and only enjoyed pre-eminence on the island of Rhodes.

Needless to say, the Sun is the most important heavenly body for the astrologer. Its qualities are summed up as follows by William Lilly. When well placed: 'Prudent, and of incomparable Judgement; of great Majesty and Stateliness, Industrious to acquire Honour and a large Patrimony, yet as willingly departing therewith againe: the Solar man usually speaks with gravity, but not many words, and those with great confidence and command of his owne affection; full of Thought, Secret, Trusty, speaks deliberately, and notwithstanding his great Heart, yet he is Affable, Tractable, and very humane to all people, one loving Sumptuousness and Magnificence, and whatsoever is honourable; no sordid thoughts can enter his heart.'

When badly placed: 'Arrogant and Proud, disdaining all men, cracking of his Pedigree, he is Pur-blind in Sight and Judgement, restless, troublesome, domineering, a meer vapour, expensive, foolish, endued with no gravity in words or soberness in Actions, a Spend-thrift, wasting his patrimony and hanging on other men's charity, yet thinks all men are bound to him, because a Gentleman borne.'

The position of the Sun is usually the key element in a person's horoscope. When someone says that he is a Gemini he means that he was born with his Sun in Gemini, even though in certain cases different factors can make another sign more prominent than the Sun sign. The Sun represents the chief formative forces in a person's character.

☽

Moon

In Babylonian mythology the Moon-god Sin was, strangely enough, the most important of the three main heavenly divinities; the other two, Shamash, the Sun, and Ishtar, Venus, were his children. In contrast to later civilisations, the Babylonians regarded the Moon as masculine and portrayed him as an old man with a long beard. His successive transformations lent him a certain mystery, and he was described as 'He whose deep heart no god can penetrate'.

In Greek mythology the Moon became the goddess Selene, sister of Helios, the Sun-god; she began her journey across the sky after her brother had finished his. One of the legends told of how she fell in love with the mortal Endymion and stole a kiss from him while he slept. Endymion asked Zeus to grant him immortality, to which Zeus agreed on condition that Endymion remain eternally asleep, and every night Selene came to gaze at the sleeping Endymion. To this day the Moon is thought to influence sleep.

Here is Lilly's description of the Moon. When well placed: 'She signifieth one of composed Manners, a soft, tender creature, a Lover of all honest and ingenious Sciences, a Searcher of, and Delighter in Novelties, naturally propense to flit and shift his Habitation, unstedfast, wholly caring for the present Times, Timorous, Prodigal, and easily frighted, however loving Peace, and to live free from the cares of this Life.'

When badly placed: 'A meer Vagabond, and idle Person, hating Labour, a Drunkard, a Sot, one of no Spirit or Forecast, delighting to live beggarly and carelessly, one content in no condition of Life, either good or ill.'

The characteristics of the Moon tend to the opposite of those of the Sun. Whereas the Sun is active, masculine, and outgoing, the Moon is passive, feminine, and retiring. Responsiveness, sensitivity, and affection are the Moon's key words.

4

The Signs of the Zodiac

The Ram, the Bull, the Heavenly Twins,
And next the Crab the Lion shines,
    The Virgin and the Scales,
The Scorpion, Archer, and Sea-Goat,
The Man that bears the Watering-Pot,
    The Fish with glittering tails.

Traditional rhyme

IN order to understand the characteristics of your own sign of the zodiac it is necessary to know the various categories into which the signs fall. First, they can be grouped under the four elements, Fire, Earth, Air, and Water – three signs to each element. The characteristics traditionally associated with the elements are as follows:

> FIRE: volatile, forceful, restless
> EARTH: dependable, static, practical
> AIR: lively, unpredictable, communicative
> WATER: emotional, sensitive, unstable

The second way in which the signs are divided is into positive and negative signs. Fire and Air are positive. Earth and Water are negative The positive signs incline the native to an active outlook, the negative ones to a passive outlook.

The third division is into Cardinal, Fixed, and Mutable signs, whose characteristics are as follows:

CARDINAL: dominating, outgoing, strong
FIXED: cautious, conservative, steadfast
MUTABLE: adaptable, versatile, changeable

It is also important to know that each sign is ruled by a planet from which it takes its characteristics. Figure 3 shows the neat scheme into which the traditional rulerships fall. As can be seen, the addition of the new planets upsets the symmetry.

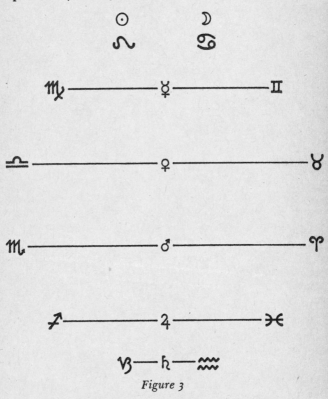

Figure 3

Now we come to the signs themselves and their characteristics, summarised in the following pages.

♈

Aries

March 21–April 20. Fire, positive, Cardinal; ruler, Mars. This is traditionally the first sign of the zodiac, since in Babylonian times the solar year began in the constellation of the Ram. The heavenly host was thought of by the early astrologers as a flock of sheep with a ram (the Sun) as its leader. Since the year began in Aries (i.e. taking the beginning of the year as the spring equinox) it was thought that the brightest star of the constellation took on the character of a ram, opening the year in much the same way as the Sun opened the day

The characteristics of the sign of Aries are, to a large extent, determined by those of its ruling planet, Mars. Since Mars was associated with the god of war, it is natural that Aries should be one of the traditional military signs, as befits its fiery element. The Arian person is forceful and self-assertive, with plenty of drive and initiative. He often has natural qualities of leadership. His singleness of purpose and determination can verge on ruthlessness, and he may make himself unpopular with others. He is fierce-tempered, passionate in love, and strong in sexual feelings.

The 17th-century astrologer, Henry Coley, in his book *Astrologiae Elimita*, said that the Sun in Aries produced 'a noble spirited soul, very courageous and valiant, delights in all War-like Actions, gains victory, and honour thereby, appears a terrour to his Enemies, and thereby makes himself famous in his Generation, some times even beyond his capacity of Birth.'

According to the ancient Greek author, Rhetorios, Aries often makes people 'bright-complexioned, long-nosed, dark-eyed, bald in front, dignified, slight of build, well-shaped, thin-legged, sweet-voiced, highminded'.

One of the most famous of typical Arians was the German soldier and statesman Otto von Bismarck who had all the strong, warlike qualities of the sign. Other famous Arians: Baudelaire, Swinburne, Thomas Jefferson, Charlie Chaplin, Adolf Hitler.

Aries Occupations

If you are an Arian and are doing a routine job, tied to an office desk and at the beck and call of other people, then you are hiding your light under a bushel. As an Arian you need an active, varied job that gives you plenty of opportunity to exercise your initiative and powers of leadership. An Arian thrives best when he is his own boss, even if it is only in a small way or involves risks and insecurity. The Aries temperament enjoys risk. A typical Aries will not be happy in a job that is too quiet and without noise and excitement he will languish. Soldiering is one of the traditional Arian activities, because it makes good use of the aggressive, martial instincts of the sign. Other suitable Arian jobs are: fireman, steelworker, butcher, professional sportsman, surgeon.

The Aries Lover

The Arian can be difficult in marriage because of the strong will and domineering character of the sign. The marriage partner of an Arian must therefore be someone who is content to take a subordinate role in the partnership, or, alternatively, who is able to stand up to the Arian partner without causing a clash of personalities. The Arian husband will probably do best with a wife who is able to make him think that he is the dominating half of the marriage, and yet at the same time is able to steer him gently in the way she wants. She must also be tolerant of his moods and capable of responding to his strong emotions. Gemini or Libra would be good signs for such a partner. The Arian wife will not usually be content with a meek husband, but will want someone who can match her strength of will and personality. A Leo husband would be a suitable choice. The Leonian is strong, yet at the same time capable of making allowances for the more difficult sides of the Arian character.

♉

Taurus

April 21–May 21. Earth, negative, Fixed; ruler, Venus. The bull was a common symbol in Middle Eastern and Mesopotamian mythology, and the naming of the constellation of Taurus is thought to derive from a Babylonian legend. The story goes that the amorous but fickle goddess, Ishtar, fell in love with Gilgamesh, the Babylonian Hercules. The latter would have nothing to do with her and, in a rage, Ishtar asked Anu, her father, to create a Bull of Heaven to destroy Gilgamesh. This her father did; and the Bull is the one that now draws the Plough (that is, the constellation of Triangulum).

Ishtar became Venus, and, perhaps because of Ishtar's connection with the Bull, Venus is the planet that rules Taurus.

Coley says that the Sun in Taurus indicates 'a good confident, bold Person, sufficiently strong, and not a little proud thereof, delighting much in opposition of others, and generally becomes a Conqueror.'

Of the physical characteristics of Taurus he says: 'It personates one of a short and thick stature, a strong body, a broad face and forehead, wide nose, great mouth, a fat short neck, short arms, thick hands, thick black hair, crisping or curling, big buttocks, and short legs, slow to anger, but if once angered not easily or suddenly reconciled again.'

Venus is the planet of love, warmth, and gentleness, and the sign of Taurus reflects these qualities. The Taurean is affectionate and kind in his dealings with others. His nature is down to earth and practical.

Oliver Cromwell had the stolid practicality of a typical Taurean. Other well-known Taureans were Balzac, Robespierre, Shakespeare and Karl Marx.

Taurus Occupations

People tend to stress the earthy qualities of the sign of Taurus. It is true that the Taurean has his feet firmly on the ground, is full of commonsense, and is painstaking and practical. But it must also be remembered that Taurus is ruled by Venus and has much of the personal warmth and understanding of the planet. The ideal occupation for the Taurean is therefore one that combines these two sides of his character. A typical Taurean would, for example, do well in medicine, where patience, commonsense, and human sympathy are needed. Taureans usually love the countryside and the outdoor life; many therefore make good farmers, foresters, and gardeners. The Taurean works well with other people and is quite content to take a 'behind-the-scenes' role. For this reason his work often does not receive its due credit.

The Taurus Lover

The Taurean needs, above all, a partner who can give him or her, a calm and ordered home life. But Taurus is also a passionate sign, and people born under it are frequently highly sexed. Therefore the ideal partner must also have strong physical passions. The Taurean dislikes emotional upsets and prefers to sort out disagreements by talking things over calmly rather than by 'clearing the air' with rows. As a husband he is very devoted to his wife and children and is content for his life to revolve around the home. He needs a wife who is capable of managing a household efficiently and who is not restless or temperamental.

The Taurean wife is unselfish and self-sacrificing. She gives out much love to her husband and family and expects much from them. Taureans go well together as partners, as do Taureans and Pisceans. Capricorn can also be a good choice as a partner.

♊

Gemini

May 22–June 21. Air, positive, Mutable; ruler, Mercury. The origin of Gemini, the Twins, like that of Taurus, is probably connected with the god Gilgamesh. It commemorates the close, twin-like friendship between Gilgamesh and Enkidu, the mischievous creature who had been fashioned from a piece of clay by the earth-goddess, Aruru.

The typical Geminian, Coley says, is 'a good disposition'd Person, affable and courteous to all, not very fortunate in any affairs, subject to the checks and controlement of others, and patiently passes over slight abuses, which none but a very mild tempered Person would be content to do.'

Physically, the Geminian has 'an upright, straight and tall body, well set and composed; a good colour though not very clear, bright eyes and good sight, long arms, fleshy hands and feet, large breast, and brown hair.'

As Mercury is the planet of the mind, so the typical Geminian is quick-witted and resourceful. He can turn his hand to many different activities, but often finds it difficult to settle for any one. He can be something of a 'Jack of all trades, master of none'. Mercury is also the planet of communication, and Geminians love to talk. Usually they make entertaining companions, but sometimes they are accused of 'liking the sound of their own voices'. They also excel in written communication. Gemini is a double sign, and the Geminian often lives a double existence, moving easily from one role to another. His faults are a tendency to be over-argumentative and to react in too intellectual a way to other people. He also inclines to insincerity, even deceptiveness. Gemini criminals tend to be confidence tricksters and imposters.

John F. Kennedy, born with his Sun in Gemini, had the intellect and speaking ability of the sign. Queen Victoria, George V, and Laurence Olivier were also born with Sun in Gemini.

Gemini Occupations

Because of the Geminian's restless, versatile nature, he is best in a job which is not too routine or humdrum. Many Geminians make admirable journalists. They like the constant movement of a reporter's life and they have the ability to create and communicate news. Short assignments suit them better than tasks that demand prolonged effort. The Geminian is not suited to heavy physical work, but he excels at skilled manual work of the lighter kind. Being a good speaker and communicator he also does well in the teaching profession. Geminians often have the gift of tongues and can make excellent translators and interpreters. They are also to be found in the commercial world where their astute minds and persuasive tongues make them good businessmen and salesmen. Geminians sometimes annoy their more solemn fellows because they appear to succeed without taking life seriously.

The Gemini Lover

The Geminian's attitude to love, like his attitude towards other aspects of life, tends to be playful and flippant. Geminians are attractive to the opposite sex, but are rarely emotionally involved at a deep level. The Geminian husband needs to be entertained and stimulated mentally.

The steady, devoted, home-loving wife is not for him. She needs to play the game of love at the same level as he does, without possessiveness or jealousy. The Geminian wife needs a colourful and amusing husband, who must not be upset when she is flattered and pleased at other men's compliments. Neither the Geminian husband nor the Geminian wife will be unfaithful as long as their partner is not too demanding. Geminians go well with other Geminians. They also go well with Arians and Librans.

♋

Cancer

June 22–July 22. Water, negative, Cardinal; ruler, Moon. Why the constellation of the Crab was so named is not known. It is ruled by the Moon, the planet of intuition, sensitivity, and emotional response.

The writer, Frederick Rolfe, alias Baron Corvo, author of *Hadrian the Seventh*, was particularly interested in Cancer, since it was his own sign. In another novel, *The Desire and Pursuit of the Whole*, he describes the sign as follows:

Under his shell, in fact, your crab is as soft as butter, and just one labyrinthine mass of the most sensitive of nerves. From which pleasing experiment [i.e. dissecting a crab] you should learn to be as merciful as God to all poor sinners born between the twenty-first of June and the twenty-fourth of July: For they are born under the constellation of Cancer; and their nature is the nature of a crab. They are the cleverest, tenderest, unhappiest, most dreadful of all men.

Clever men and dreadful men are not invariably unhappy, but crab-men are all three – excepting on one sole condition. That condition is their union with a Saturnian, born between the twentieth of December and the twenty-first of January, who is their diametrical opposite and complement, soft outside, hard within.

Rolfe himself typified these Cancerian characteristics.

He was sensitive in the extreme and took offence at the slightest provocation. At the same time he preserved a cold exterior – the 'hard shell' of the crab. Cancerians also like to feel part of a family, whether it is their own or some substitute for it. They often identify with some family-like organisation such as a church or political party. In Rolfe's case it was the Roman Catholic Church that fulfilled his need.

Julius Caesar, the Duke of Windsor, and Edward Heath were also born with Sun in Cancer.

Cancer Occupations

Though the Cancerian likes to feel that he is a member of a family he is not a good mixer and his relations with other people are often difficult. The most suitable occupation for him is one in which he can operate on his own. Writing novels, as Rolfe did, is an ideal Cancerian activity, combining independence with an opportunity to exercise the artistic gifts and intuitive understanding of the sign. Indeed any form of independent artistic activity – painting, sculpture, composing, photography – is suitable for the Cancerian. Cancer is also a water sign and is ruled by the Moon which has a strong connection with the sea. The Cancerian, therefore, often has a strong affinity for the sea and all occupations connected with it – diver, sailor, fisherman, marine biologist, lighthouse keeper.

The Cancer Lover

A love-affair with a Cancerian is likely to be a difficult business. Cancerians do not release their emotions easily and when they do they can still withdraw quickly into their shell if they feel injured or slighted. But, although the Cancerian is a difficult partner, Rolfe was possibly exaggerating when he said that a Capricorn was the only possible match. Capricorn is certainly a good choice, but

Taurus would also be suitable. The home-loving qualities of the Taurean would appeal to a Cancerian, and the Venusian warmth and sympathy would draw the crab out of his shell. Above all a Cancerian should avoid marrying another Cancerian. The Cancer wife is easier to please than the Cancer husband and will fall very happily into the role of mother. In spite of the difficulties of the sign, the Cancerian will make a loyal and devoted partner if the right match is found.

♌
Leo

July 23–August 23. Fire, positive, Fixed; ruler, Sun.
The lion is king of the beasts and the Sun is king of the heavens; therefore it is natural that the Sun has always been identified with the lion. The fact that the sign of Leo coincides with the height of summer, when the Sun is at its most powerful, probably accounts for the naming of the constellation.

According to Coley, the Leonian is 'A strong, well proportioned portly person, of a very Sanguine Complexion, a light brown, or yellowish Hair, a full Face, and a large Eye, sometimes a mark or scarr in the Face, a very just Person, faithful to his friend, punctual in the performance of his promise, yet delights to take his pleasure, is ambitious of honour, whether in War, or otherwise; and usually promotes all things in order thereunto.'

The person born with his Sun in Leo is almost invariably a strong personality with a taste for leadership. The sign has always been associated with monarchs and rulers. The faults that can afflict the sign are conceit, vanity, pomposity, and lust for power. At his best, however, the Leonian is a thoroughly likeable person, warm, and outgoing, with a great capacity to attract the friendship, loyalty, and respect of others.

Napoleon was a Leo who misused his talents. The same applies to Mussolini. Princess Margaret, also born under the sign, has the more positive Leonian qualities.

Leo Occupations

The Leonian is best in any occupation where his natural capacity for leadership and organisation can be expressed. He is the ideal committee chairman – strong, authoritative, and able to command the obedience and loyalty of others through arousing their respect and affection. He does not usually work well on his own, because he needs to feel that he is leading and commanding others. He does not focus his mind easily on the details of a task; his talent is for laying down general outlines of policy for others to follow. Politics is a natural outlet for the Leonian talents. Another characteristic of Leonian types is that they like to project their personalities, even to 'show off'. Hence they make good actors. They also like anything to do with finery, decoration and magnificence. They often have a fondness for precious stones and are frequently found as jewellers and goldsmiths.

The Leo Lover

As a lover, the Leonian is uninhibited, passionate, and domineering, and needs a partner who is able to match the Leonian strength of personality or else is happy to be subservient. Aries can be a good choice as a partner. The hot-blooded, passionate Arian will give the necessary emotional and sexual fulfilment. The two signs would also stimulate each other mentally and share a desire to create a beautiful home, which is an important requirement for the Leo. Occasionally the sparks may fly, but that is natural and desirable in a marriage between two people of the fire element. An alternative would be someone born under Libra, who would complement rather than match the Leonian qualities, providing a calm and modest foil to the outgoing, assertive Leo.

♍

Virgo

August 24–September 23. Earth, negative, Mutable; ruler, Mercury.

The Sun appeared in Virgo at harvest time. Hence it was natural to associate this constellation with a female Earth-goddess type of figure, who later became transformed into a demure maiden.

Here is what the 20th-century astrologer, Vivian Robson, says about Virgo in her *Student's Textbook of Astrology*, published in 1922. (The words in capitals are those closely connected with the symbol of the Virgin; those with an initial capital letter are suggested by the earthy, mutable, Mercurial qualities of the sign; and those in italics are the qualities gained from proximity to Leo, the sign preceding Virgo in the zodiac.)

Cool, Practical, Discriminating, very Critical, *often destructively so*, Impassive, Faddy Over Little Things, very Inquisitive, MODEST, RETIRING, faithful, Intellectual, *strong opinions*, fond of Art, Literature, Science and Mathematics, fond of collecting, Good Memory and Reasoning Power, not very original, slow to anger and forgiveness, QUIET, Persuasive, Very Good At Detail Work, fond of Gardening, Reading, COOKING AND NEEDLEWORK, etc.; often servile to *rich and distinguished people, fond of telling people their faults*, worry over Little Things but brave in emergency, insist on respect, often rather OLD-MAIDISH.

This sums up the traditional Virgoan characteristics. The sign is, like Gemini, ruled by Mercury; but whereas Gemini represents the planet in its more abstract, intellectual form, Virgo represents it in its practical form. On the positive side, Virgoans are hard-working, meticulous, conscientious, methodical, and skilful with their hands. On the negative side, they tend to be aloof and often find it hard to make friends.

Tolstoy had the earthy nature and vigorous mind of the sign. Another famous writer who shared the sign was Goethe. More recent Virgoans: Lyndon Johnson, Peter Sellers.

Virgo Occupations

The foremost asset of the Virgoan is his capacity to take great pains over detail. He is a perfectionist in all that he undertakes and has a passion for cleanliness, orderliness, and neatness. He is not usually endowed with great imagination and hence is better as an administrator rather than initiator of policies. He is somewhat reserved and lacks the charismatic personality of the Leonian. Hence he rarely comes to the fore as a leader, but rather acts as a prop and helper to public figures, often exercising a great deal of power in this way. 'Grey eminence' is the term used by those who are jealous of his influence. Though intelligent, he does not lay too much value in mental attainments, and often prefers physical work. He is good at doing skilful, meticulous work with his hands. Watchmaking is the kind of job at which he excels; indeed any kind of skilled craft will suit him. Virgoans with more intellectual inclinations will be good as secretaries or accountants. They also do well as doctors and nurses because of their interest in health and hygiene.

The Virgo Lover

In love the Virgoan is often cool and inhibited. Love is an untidy emotion; and the Virgoan, with his passion for tidiness, finds difficulty in fitting it into his scheme of things. This can take the form of a healthy modesty, or it can turn into an over-sensitive, untouchable attitude. The Virgoan often has a detached and unemotional approach towards sex. This can lead to promiscuity and a callous attitude towards the potential partner. But the Virgoan has emotions like everyone else, and once committed will be faithful and loving. He will not be swept off his feet by another person; his love will grow slowly, but its roots will be strong. The Virgoan husband or wife is stable, conscientious and interested in the home, as well as being kind and thoughtful towards the partner. Virgo types are happiest when married to members of their own sign, but Capricorn or Taurus would also be suitable.

♎

Libra

September 24–October 23. Air, positive, Cardinal; ruler, Venus.

The month in which the sign of Libra falls was, in Babylonian tradition, the one in which the gods fixed the fates according their judgement of mortals. Judgement implied weighing and balancing; hence the constellation governing the month came to be referred to as that of the scales.

The Sun in Libra, according to Coley, 'gives an upright, strait Body, an Oval face, a ruddy, cheerful Complexion, light hair, and a full Eye, sometimes Pimples in the Face; but (if Authors may be credited, and there is both reason and experience to confirm it) the Sun in *Libra*, signifies a very unfortunate person in all, or most of his Actions, especially in War-like affairs; for therein he is sure to come off with dishonour, if he escapes other dangers, unless his significator be befriended by some potent planet . . .'

Not all astrologers would agree that Libra is an 'unfortunate' sign, but Coley is right in saying that Librans do not take to war-like actions. Librans are fond of harmony and balance, and fight shy of any kind of conflict or disagreement. If ever a Libran is involved in an argument he will go out of his way to bring about a compromise. This makes him popular and generally surrounded by many friends.

Libra, like Taurus, is ruled by Venus; but whereas Taurus is an Earth sign, Libra comes under the Air element. The Libran shares the warmth and companionability of the Taurean, but he is at the same time quicker-witted and resolute. His dislike of conflict often makes him unable to face up to difficulties. Another common failing of the Libran is laziness.

Gandhi's devotion to non-violence was typical of his sign of Libra, though his asceticism was not a typical Libran quality – most Librans like their creature comforts. Other famous Librans: Nelson, Annie Besant, Hindenburg, Ramsay MacDonald, Pope Paul VI.

Libra Occupations

The Libran always works well with other people, but is not particularly good as a leader, since he shies away from confrontations or unpleasant conflicts of any kind. In fact he is always trying to patch up quarrels between other people and 'pour oil on troubled waters'. Hence Librans often make good diplomats and arbitrators. He loves beauty and pleasant surroundings and often has creative gifts. Some Librans make good interior decorators, others make good painters and sculptors. He is not good at rough, manual work or anything that involves working in ugly surroundings. If he is in trade he should be a tailor, jeweller, art dealer, or anything that has to do with selling beautiful objects.

The Libra Lover

In love, the Libran is the opposite of the cool Virgoan – he is 'in love with love', constantly seeking out amorous experiences, and full of charm and attraction for the opposite sex. To be at his or her best the Libran needs the constant moral support and love of a partner. The Libran husband or wife is very easy to live with. The Libran very rarely quarrels, as this upsets the balance and harmony that are all-important to members of the sign. It is therefore not a good idea for a Libran to marry someone who likes a tempestuous relationship, full of rows and passionate reconciliations. A Taurean or another Libran would be a good choice.

♏

Scorpio

October 24–November 22. Water, negative, Fixed; rulers, Mars and Pluto.

The scorpion was a common figure in Babylonian mythology, though why the constellation was so named remains a mystery.

Here are the characteristics of the Scorpionic type according to the 19th-century astrologer Zadkiel (whose real name was Richard James Morrison): 'A well-set form of middle stature, rather corpulent; swarthy complexion, black, curling hair, broad and plain face. The temper is very unsociable and rash; they are generally revengeful, ungrateful, quarrelsome and wicked; yet of good genius and ready apprehension, excelling in mystery etc.'

Scorpio shares with Aries the characteristics of being ruled by Mars. Scorpio is under the element of water, signifying emotion. Hence the forcefulness of Mars tends to be expressed in Scorpio through emotional channels. The Scorpionic type is temperamental, aggressive, and ambitious. He often possesses great powers of leadership, though he tends to command obedience by arousing fear rather than affection. He has not the outgoing warmth of Leo. You never quite know where you stand with a Scorpio. There are deep layers of complexity in his personality which can never be completely fathomed. The sign has always been associated with sexuality, and the Scorpionic person is generally endowed with strong sexual instincts. Traditionally, Scorpio rules the genital organs. It is also associated with speech, and Scorpionic types often have powerful, resonant, commanding voices.

General de Gaulle, with his powers of leadership, aloofness, and prickly nature, has many of the Scorpionic characteristics. Richard Burton displays the artistic gifts of the sign. Martin Luther, another Scorpio, had the characteristic Scorpionic courage and emotional intensity.

Scorpio Occupations

Scorpio and Aries, because of their Mars rulership, are the traditional military signs. Scorpios, like Aries types, have the physical stamina, powers of leadership, and aggressive instincts that make good soldiers. Because of their ability to project themselves through speech, Scorpios often make successful actors – Richard Burton for example. They also make good politicians and barristers – careers which demand forceful speech and the ability to enjoy an argument. Margaret Hone, in her *Modern Text Book of Astrology*, says that the Mars rulership gives the Scorpio a desire to 'cut, penetrate and to probe'. Hence 'He will be well placed as a doctor or preferably a surgeon who cuts into the body, or a psychologist who probes into the mental states of the unconscious self, endeavouring to bring to the surface and to get rid of what was hidden. His ability to search for what is hidden and his persistence in tracking it down make him a good detective.' Scorpio is also a water sign, which means that the native will love the sea and will be attracted towards occupations concerned with it. He may also incline towards careers involving the arts.

The Scorpio Lover

The Scorpionic type, as I have said, is highly sexed and very passionate. But his sexual feelings are usually matched by a corresponding depth of emotion. He loves with an intensity unequalled by any other sign. Hence he can be violently jealous and vindictive if he feels that his partner has betrayed him. The Scorpionic husband can be dictatorial and domineering and needs a wife who is able to stand up to him. The Scorpio wife, similarly, needs a strong husband whom she can respect. A weak one will soon become hen-pecked. Capricorn and Taurus are both good matches for Scorpio.

♐

Sagittarius

November 23–December 21. Fire, positive, Mutable; ruler, Jupiter.

This sign is usually represented by a centaur firing an arrow. In the early days of Babylonian astrology, Sagittarius and the preceding sign of Scorpio were grouped together. In many early illustrations the centaur has a scorpion's tail, with another scorpion below. The double sign was associated with the warlike god Ninurta. The precise origin of Sagittarius has, however, not been discovered.

The sign of Sagittarius says Coley, 'gives a tall well-proportioned comly person, with an Oval Visage, a curious sanguine Complexion, and a light brown Hair; for qualities and disposition, a very lofty proud spirited Person, aiming at great things, and too severe in the exercise of his power; yet some honourable exploits are performed by him, which adds much to his commendation, and renders him a very noble humoured Person.'

The sign is ruled by, and takes much of its character from, its ruling planet, Jupiter. It is from the Latin word for Jupiter that we derive our word 'jovial', which describes one aspect of the planet's character. The Sagittarian is thus, among other things, a person of sanguine, cheerful, friendly disposition. But he also takes on the planet's qualities of intellect and capacity for deep thought. He is both physically and mentally restless. The arrow represents his love of freedom, movement, and quest. The sign comes under the fire element, denoting that Sagittarians are of quick temper and strong passions. They are also renowned for their love of sport and the outdoors. Because of his independent nature the Sagittarian finds it hard to be subservient, or to make partnerships on an equal basis. He also has a tendency to become boisterous and self-assertive. Winston Churchill had the independence and thrusting determination of the sign. Other famous Sagittarians were Beethoven, Berlioz, Disraeli, and Walt Disney.

Sagittarius Occupations

Wanderlust is one of the Sagittarian characteristics, and anyone born under this sign will be very unhappy if he is in a job that ties him down, especially if it is an entirely indoor job, for the Sagittarian hates to be confined between four walls for long. Travelling salesman, bus driver, taxi-driver, lorry driver, pilot, air hostess – all these are occupations which would suit the Sagittarian. Margaret Hone writes: 'He is better when both body and mind have equal freedom of development.' Ideally he should have a job that stretches him in both of these ways, for the Sagittarian has a profound and thoughtful side to his character through the influence of Jupiter. His 'jovial' qualities also make him good at dealing with other people, and his job should involve plenty of human contact.

The Sagittarius Lover

In love, the Sagittarian can be difficult and cause many headaches and heartaches for his opposite number. The Fire element in him makes him passionate and ardent, but the Mutable quality of Sagittarius makes him liable to sudden changes of mind. His desire for freedom makes him resist emotional ties, and marriage will often be a difficult step for him. Neither the Sagittarian husband nor the Sagittarian wife will be content to remain preoccupied entirely with the partner. The stimulus of social life and friends will also be necessary, and the partner must be prepared to go along with this. Gemini or Aquarius are good mates for the Sagittarian.

♑

Capricorn

December 22–January 20. Earth, negative, Cardinal; ruler, Saturn.

The sign of Capricorn is usually shown as a goat with a fish-tail. This represents one of the forms in which appeared the Babylonian god Ea, who lived in the sea and emerged only at rare intervals to teach civilisation to mankind. One of his titles was 'antelope of the subterranean ocean'.

The 4th-century Roman writer, Porphyry, mentions the doctrine that souls descend to earth in Cancer and begin their ascent to heaven in Capricorn. Cancer, the warm, moist sign of the summer tropic, represents the pull of material things. Capricorn, a winter sign, is stony and hard; it is here that man rises above material attractions by deep and arduous thought. This bears out the common view of Capricorn as a rather grim, stoical sign.

Coley says that the Sun in Capricorn 'usually represents a mean statur'd Person, of a sickly Complexion, Brown Hair, not curling, an Oval Face, a spare thin Body, not decently composed, but rather a disproportion in the Members thereof; for disposition, very just in his Actions, thereby gaining love and friendship; sometimes passionate, a favourer of the Female sex; and in general, a reasonable good humoured Person to those he hath Conversation withal.'

Although Saturn was thought to cast a gloomy light over the sign of Capricorn, it is now thought by astrologers that the restraint and discipline of Saturn can often be beneficial. This can be seen in the endurance, courage, and powers of concentration displayed by the Capricornian. It is true that he tends to lack a sense of humour, but his good qualities often make up for this. He is like the mountain goat who prefers the arduous and stony path, and by it often reaches greater heights than his fellows.

The Emperor Augustus had the fortitude and endurance in the fact of hardships and stress that are characteristic of Capricorn. So proud was he of his sign that he had a coin struck bearing the goat emblem. Other famous people with Sun in Capricorn: Gladstone, Joan of Arc, Charles Clore.

Capricorn Occupations

The Capricornian excels in activities that demand discipline, toughness, and endurance. He might do well, for example, as a lifeboatman, member of a mountain rescue team, or a policeman. He has a tremendous capacity for hard work, and will often rise to the top by sheer persistence, surprising those who are inclined to dismiss him as a plodder. But he does not generally do well where a great deal of imagination is called for, and he is better at carrying out other people's plans than originating any of his own. Also he is not very good at dealing with people. The more intellectual Capricorn will be suited to organisational work in business or the Civil Service.

The Capricorn Lover

'Look before you leap' is a favourite Capricornian maxim, and this applies to his love life as well as to everything else he does. He will enter very slowly into a love affair, and his partner must not expect him to bare his soul at the first meeting. Even when his emotions are fully engaged with another person he will remain somewhat reticent and his feelings will be expressed gravely and unflippantly. Loyalty is one of the Capricornian's strongest points, and once he has entered into marriage he will be faithful and devoted. This applies to Capricornians of both sexes. Capricornians are well suited to members of their own sign. Cancer is also a good match.

∽∽∽

Aquarius

January 21–February 19. Air, positive, Fixed; rulers, Saturn and Uranus.

Aquarius, the water-pourer, is so named because of the heavy rainfall that occurred in Babylonia in January, the month when the Sun was in this constellation.

The sign was traditionally ruled by Saturn, and therefore takes on some of the characteristics of the planet. But modern astrologers tend to regard it as being more under the dominion of Uranus, from which it is believed to take on a disruptive, revolutionary character. It is this aspect of Aquarius that probably appeals to the 'Aquarian Age' fraternity.

Coley says of Aquarius: 'The Sun in Aquarius describes a Person of all middle stature, a corpulent Body, decently composed, a round full Face, a light brown Hair, and generally clear complexion; the disposition moderately good, but subject to Ostentation, and desirous to bear rule, but free from malicious Actions against any Person.'

The Aquarian combines Saturnian and Uranian characteristics. He is, like the Saturnian Capricorn, serious and reserved. But, whereas the Capricornian is conservative and distrustful of change, the Aquarian is impatient of traditional restraints. Another characteristic is that he finds it easier to love humanity as a whole than to establish a relationship with one person. Aquarius is also associated with science, logical thinking, and rationality.

Charles Dickens had the humanitarianism of the sign. A less typical Aquarian was Frederick the Great of Prussia, though it might be argued that his military exploits were disruptive and Uranian in character. Harold Macmillan and Yehudi Menuhin were also born with their Sun in Aquarius.

Aquarius Occupations

Unlike his neighbour, Capricorn, Aquarius is very much of an innovator with a leaning towards what is new and revolutionary; but he shares with Capricorn the Saturn rulership and the discipline that goes with it. Hence he is best in occupations that combine these two characteristics. The work of an inventor is possibly the most typical Aquarian activity, but all branches of science appeal to this sign. The Aquarian has a strongly altruistic side to his character and many Aquarians do well in the fields of social work and charity. Politics of a radical nature also appeal to them. Aquarians are rebels by nature and should not be placed in situations where they are expected to 'toe the line'.

The Aquarius Lover

Because his emotional involvement tends to be with humanity as a whole the Aquarian tends to find difficulty in developing a love relationship. When he does develop one he is apt to remain rather detached, and it is important for the partner not to be emotionally demanding. The partnership should be based on a common interest in intellectual pursuits, social objectives, or any shared activity outside the home. The Aquarian husband or wife must also be allowed plenty of freedom to be alone at times and to develop his or her own interests. Two Aquarians will make a good match. Gemini is also a good choice.

♓

Pisces

February 20–March 20. Water, negative, Mutable; rulers, Jupiter and Neptune.

In early Babylonian zodiacs this constellation is shown as two fishes connected by a string, representing the two goddesses ruling the two Mesopotamian rivers, the Tigris and Euphrates. It is uncertain why this constellation should be connected with the rivers. Possibly it was to do with the height of the water after the rainfall of the previous month.

The Sun in Pisces, says Coley, 'gives a Person rather short than tall of stature, a round Face, and an indifferent good Complexion, a light brown Hair, sometimes flaxen, a reasonable plump or corpulent Body, a general lover of the Female-sex, and his own delights and pleasures; addicted to Gaming, and Feasting, many times to his own detriment; yet a person very harmless to others, injures none but himself by too much extravagant expense and prodigality, so far as his substance will extend.'

Pisces is, like Scorpio and Aquarius, ruled by an 'old' and a 'new' planet. It takes from Jupiter the qualities of intellect and insight, but is considered by many modern astrologers to be more strongly influenced by Neptune, the planet of sensitivity and intuition.

The Piscean, though sensitive and intelligent, is somewhat passive and negative in his personality and approach to life. He shies away from action and decisions, and tends to drift through a world of dreams and fantasy. This is possibly why many poets, novelists, artists, and musicians are Pisceans. Chopin, with his highly strung temperament and musical genius, was typical of the sign. Other Pisceans are Einstein, 'Buffalo Bill', Harold Wilson.

Pisces Occupations

Pisceans, because of their dreamy nature, do not generally excel in highly practical activities. Their natural milieu is art. Any form of creative activity suits them. The Jupiter rulership also gives them an interest in religion and they are often to be found as ministers. Their sensitive, intuitive nature often makes them good mediums. Anything to do with the sea attracts them, because of the watery nature of the sign. Their fluid, flexible personalities enable them to slide easily into different roles; hence they make good character actors and impersonators.

The Pisces Lover

The Piscean drifts easily into love, but he also drifts easily out of it again, and he should beware of entering lightly into marriage. His approach to love will be intense and ecstatic, and his charm and ability to express his feelings will make him irresistible to the object of his love. But there is always the danger that his affections will switch suddenly to someone else. The Piscean is, however, a dependent creature, who leans on those with more practical ability than himself, and if he finds a partner who is prepared to make up for his deficiencies he will not readily look elsewhere. The Piscean woman fits easily into the role of wife, provided that her husband is not too fussy about a tidy home; the Piscean husband, however, tends to leave too much to his wife and to retreat into his own rather unreal world. The best partner for the Piscean is someone who is practical and also able to supply the warmth of emotion that the Piscean needs. Taurus is a good choice.

5
The Houses

No star ever rose
And set, without some influence somewhere.

Owen Meredith, *Lucile*

THE best way to explain the function of the houses in relation to the signs and planets is as follows: the planets are the forces that act on human beings; the signs are *how* they act; and the houses are *where* they act. That is to say, the houses represent the departments of everyday life in which the celestial forces make themselves apparent. It is to the houses that the astrologer looks if he wishes to answer 'mundane' questions such as whether a native will be rich, how many children he will have, or how good his health will be.

The houses, like the signs, are divided into categories which make characterisation easier. The three groups into which the houses fall are angular, succedent, and cadent. The first group comprises the houses that occupy the angles, i.e. the ascendant, lowest heaven, descendant, and mid-heaven. These are the 1st, 4th, 7th, and 10th houses. The angular houses denote power and initiative. Planets are thought to exercise a stronger influence when they are close to the angles in a horoscope. The succedent houses, the 2nd, 5th, 8th, and 11th, are more passive, signifying result, rather than initiation. The cadent houses, the 3rd, 6th, 9th, and 12th, denote spreading and dispersal of energies.

Not all astrologers agree on which houses govern which departments of life, but the following attributions would be generally accepted.

The 1st house refers to the personality of the native whose horoscope is being studied. His appearance, manner, physical characteristics, and outlook on life will all come under this house. It also denotes childhood environment.

The 2nd house has to do with money and possessions and the kinds of object with which a person likes to surround himself.

The 3rd house, like the third sign, Gemini, refers to mental activity and communication. For example, letters and visits would come under this house. It also refers to close relatives, other than parents, such as brothers and sisters.

The 4th house reflects the character of the sign of Cancer, denoting the protectiveness of the parental home and the womb. As a logical step from this, it also refers to hereditary characteristics.

The 5th house is the house of creativity. Hence sexuality, procreation, parenthood, and children come under this house. It also governs creative activity in the artistic sphere.

The 6th house refers primarily to the native's state of health. It is also the house of his servants and subordinates.

The 7th house has similar associations to the seventh sign, Libra, the sign of harmony, ruled by Venus, the planet of love. Hence the 7th house is the house of marriage as well as of partnerships. It is also, paradoxically, the house of enemies.

The 8th house is the house of death. Possibly through association of ideas it also governs inheritances. Another area governed by the 8th house is sex as a motive force rather than as a creative process.

The 9th house takes its character from the corresponding sign of Sagittarius. As the arrow implies flight and distance, so the 9th house governs travel and the urge of wanderlust. It also refers to inner travel – mental and spiritual exploration.

The 10th house is the house of vocation and career. All matters concerning a native's job and daily work come under this house.

The 11th house is the house of social objectives and causes, just as the eleventh sign, Aquarius, is the sign governing altruism. Friendships also come under this house.

The 12th house is a rather gloomy house. It governs difficulties, restrictions, seclusion, imprisonment, and accidents.

6

Applying the Principles

It was well said of Plotinus that the stars were
significant, but not efficient.

Sir Walter Raleigh

WE have seen what the planets, signs, and houses signify.
Now let us see how they work in practice by looking at a
sample horoscope. The one shown in Figure 4 is that of
Charles, Prince of Wales, born on November 14, 1948.

The divisions around the outer edge of the circle are the
signs of the zodiac. The numbered segments inside are the
houses, and the symbols placed irregularly around the
inner rim are those of the planets. Now, before we see what
the horoscope tells us about the Prince, let us follow the
steps an astrologer would go through in casting a horoscope of this type.

The equipment he would need would be a table of the
planetary positions for the year in question, called an
ephemeris, and a table of houses for different parts of the
world. First, by reference to the table of houses, he finds
out in which sign falls the ascendant, that is the boundary
of the first house. In this case he would see that it is 5° 30
minutes in Leo. So he marks the divisions of Leo so that
the horizontal line and the arrow on the left of the chart
fall 5.30° from the line marking the beginning of Leo.
The cusps of all the other signs can then be marked in,
each 30° from the last. He then draws in the symbols of
the signs in their appropriate places.

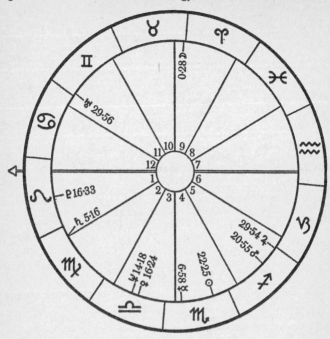

Figure 4

Next come the planets. To find their positions he refers to the ephemeris, and then enters each one. The Sun goes at 22.25° in Scorpio, the Moon at 0.28° in Aries, and so on. Next he plots the planetary aspects, that is the angles formed by the planets one to another. The aspects, divided into good and bad ones, are as follows:

Good

Conjunction ☌ This is usually beneficial, but can be harmful in certain cases; for example, Saturn and Venus together could mean that the native's emotions were stifled by the restrictions of Saturn.

Sextile ✳ This is formed when two planets make an angle of 60° with the centre of the chart. It is invariably beneficial.

Trine △ This is an angle of 120° and is particularly strong when there is a 'grand trine', that is three planets at intervals of 120° around the chart.

Bad

Opposition ☍ An angle of 180°. This is a negative aspect, usually signifying two forces depleting each other, resulting in weakness.

Square □ An angle of 90°. This is bad in a more positive sense than the opposition. It signifies tension and can act as a catalyst, spurring the individual on to overcome his difficulties and attain great achievements.

When the astrologer has calculated the aspects he will have completed the technical part of his task. Now he has to set about interpreting what he sees in the horoscope. This is where the really difficult part of astrology begins. In front of him the astrologer has a mass of interrelated data, and he has to sort it all out and arrange it in an ordered fashion so that he ends up with a description of the person whose chart he is studying

In order to do this he relies on the astrological tradition – a skeleton of standard interpretations of the basic terms in the horoscope. But as no two horoscopes are the same the astrologer must also be able to use his intuition and imagination to put the flesh on the skeleton and give a real picture of the person. There are many astrological text books from which the amateur astrologer can interpret a horoscope simply by looking up the meaning of all the basic combinations in the chart. But the professional astrologer must know how to read a chart off the cuff.

The process is rather like the one that a psychoanalyst goes through. The patient on the couch has told him, shall we say, a series of dreams, full of apparently disconnected symbols and meanings. In order to interpret these the analyst has to rely on what he has read in Jung's and Freud's books on dream interpretation, plus his own intuitive conclusions about the dreams.

Each psychoanalyst probably has his own system of interpretation, and so has every astrologer, but there are various stock ways of arranging the data in the chart. One perfectly good way is to look first at the Sun sign, Moon sign, and ascendant to determine the general characteristics of the native; then to examine the positions and aspects of each planet in turn to arrive at his particular idiosyncracies. So let us follow this procedure with the Prince of Wales and see what conclusions we reach.

Sun in ♏ in 4th

The Sun in Scorpio signifies that the Prince has a strong, sensitive, emotional character, with the ability to feel passionately as well as to act with swiftness and determination. Scorpionic types are also known for their ability to project themselves through speech. The position of the Sun in the 4th house shows that he is very home- and family-oriented, with firm loyalties to his parents.

The only significant aspect of the Sun is a square to Pluto, which is in the first house. This means that he has a conflict between his own ambitions and his loyalty to his family.

Moon in ♉ in 9th

The Moon, the planet of emotional response, being situated in Taurus means that he will get on best with people who are warm, easy-going, and down-to-earth.

The Moon's opposition to Mercury means that his social relationships will not always coincide with his intellectual interests, and he may find a conflict here. The Moon forms a grand trine with Jupiter and Saturn, which is extremely strong and beneficial. It means that the emotional, intellectual, and practical sides of his nature will work together in complete harmony.

The Moon is also sextile to Uranus. This could mean that he is subject to sudden fits of restlessness and wanderlust.

Ascendant in ♌

Leo is, par excellence, the sign of kings and rulers. Therefore, in his personality and outward behaviour the Prince will always live up to his position. He will be masterful, decisive, and determined. He will also be fond of a good show of ceremony. In his relations with other people he will be warm and friendly, and will always inspire loyalty and affection.

Mercury in ♏ in 4th

Mercury, the planet of intellect, is placed in Scorpio, which signifies, among others things, speech, in the 4th house, which signifies the home. I would interpret this to mean that Charles derives the greatest *intellectual* stimulation from *conversation* with members of his own *family*.

The sextile to Saturn means that he will have a controlled, tidy, disciplined mind, with great powers of concentration.

Venus in ♎ in 3rd

The fact that Venus is in its own sign of Libra means that the influence of this planet will be particularly strong, giving him a warm disposition and a love of beauty, harmony, and conviviality. Taking planet, sign, and house, in that order, the interpretation is that his *close friendships* will be *harmonious* and find their expression in *intellectual* communion.

The conjunction with Neptune means that he will be fond of everything to do with the sea.

The sextile to Mars means that he will enter into his friendships with warmth and enthusiasm.

The sextile to Pluto means that his friendships will suddenly erupt or blossom after an initial period of inhibition.

Mars in ♐ in 5th

Once again, interpreting planet, sign, and house, we get: *drive* will express itself in *restless* ways and will be manifest in *creative* areas – i.e. the Prince will seek release of tension in the pursuit of artistic activities.

Jupiter in ♐ in 5th

Here again we have a planet in its own sign. This reinforces the interpretation of Mars's position. It means that his *thoughtful, philosophical* side will seek *adventure* through *creativity*. The opposition with Uranus means a conflict between his creative interests and his social obligations.

Saturn in ♍ in 1st

This position indicates that the Prince is given to rigorous neatness in in his dress, appearance, and habits. This can be seen from the fact that Saturn, the planet of discipline, is placed in Virgo, the sign of neatness and meticulousness, in the 1st house, the house of the person.

Uranus in ♊ in 11th

The planet of suddenness is placed in the sign of communication in the house of friendship. This is another indication of the sudden way in which friendships are likely to develop.

Neptune in ♎ in 3rd

This position means that the intuitive side of his nature, represented by Neptune, will find its outlet in a feeling for beauty, indicated by Libra, which will reveal itself through communication, denoted by the 3rd house. One interpretation of this might be a love of the more communicative arts, such as acting.

Pluto in ♌ in 1st

Long pent-up forces will release themselves in regal ways in outward behaviour – i.e. the Prince will find new confidence and discover new resources within himself as he takes on fresh responsibilities.

Here then is the picture we get of Charles's character and personality from his horoscope. It is possible to draw up similar charts, not only for individuals, but for events, such as the formation of a society, the signing of a treaty, the launching of a ship, or a declaration of independence. The chart in each case gives general indications of what forces, beneficial or adverse, will operate in the life of an individual or the duration of an enterprise.

But so far we have not looked at the predictive side of astrology – which is what the average person usually thinks of when the word 'astrology' is mentioned. In order to make predictions about an individual it is necessary first to have drawn up a birth chart such as the one we have just examined. This is then used as a basis for forecasting the future.

There are two main methods of prediction. The first is by the use of what is known as the 'progressed' horoscope. This is a system based on the idea that every day after a person's birth represents a year of his life. Supposing you wanted to find out what the year 1980 held in store for Prince Charles. Nineteen eighty is 32 years from his birth date, so according to the 'day for a year' theory it would be represented by a day 32 days from November 14, that is December 16. You would draw up a chart of the planetary positions for that day, bearing in mind that different times of day represent different times of year. Having done this you would then compare the 'progressed' planetary positions with the 'radical' ones, i.e. those in the birth horoscope.

If you found that the progressed Saturn was in opposition to the radical Sun this would be a bad sign, indicating that the native would pass through a period of frustration. If, on the other hand, the progressed Jupiter formed a trine with the radical Sun, it would be a good sign, indicating a fruitful and creative period.

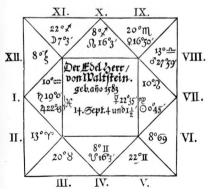

1. *Above*. The Zodiac.

2. *Left*. The horoscope which Kepler is said to have cast for Albrecht von Wallenstein (1583–1634).

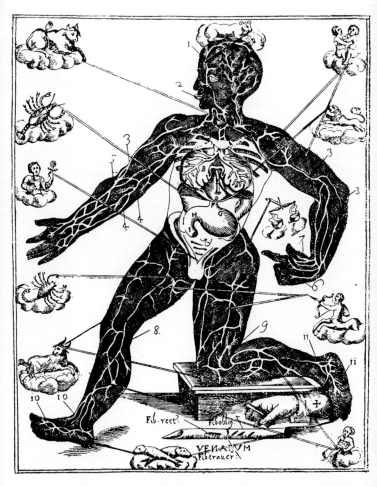

3. Two illustrations showing the harmony of the relation between the macrocosm and the microcosm, man. *Above*, from *Armonia astro-medico-anatomica* by Francesco Minniti, Venice, 1690. *Right*, from Athanasius Kircher *Mundus Subterraneus*, Amsterdam, 1678.

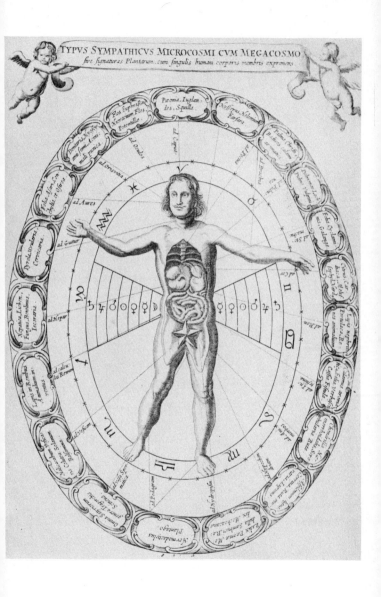

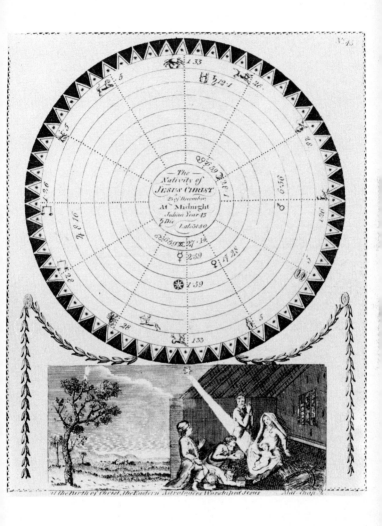

4. Horoscopes cast by Sibly in *The Celestial Science of Astrology*.
Above, the horoscope of Jesus Christ. *Left*, the horoscopes of Henry
VIII, Edward VI, Mary I, Elizabeth I, and the Earl of Essex.

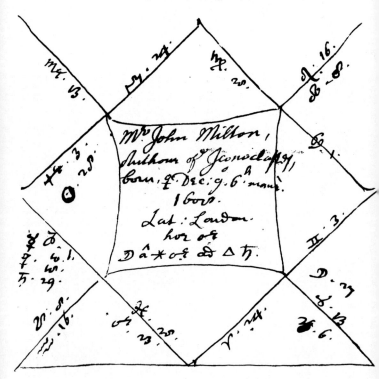

5. *Above*. The horoscope of John Milton, cast by John Gadbury.
6. *Above right*. The astrological clock at Hampton Court Palace.
7. *Below right*. A miniature from the manuscript of the astronomical and astrological treatise of Abd-Er-Rahman El-Sufi.

8. *Above*. An early engraving of an astrologer casting a horoscope.

9. *Below*. The cause of the crush in Grand Central Station, New York, is the first American installation of Astroflash, a computer programmed to deliver astrological horoscopes and forecasts. There is another Astroflash in Paris, and both were programmed by French astrologer, André Barbault.

7

A Short History of Astrology

The history of astrology is the history of the successive transformations of man's attitude to Nature.

Dane Rudhyar, *The Astrology of Personality*

IN Babylonia, where astrology began, astrological knowledge was regarded as an important part of a man's education. It was said, for example, as a proof of the indolence of King Ninus that 'he saw no star, nor seeing it took note'. The less educated classes worshipped the stars in a cruder way, looking on them as deities, but everyone was familiar with the planetary and constellation figures, which appeared on a variety of artifacts, from seal-cylinders to boundary-stones. Babylonian astrology was, at first, used only to predict general events such as natural disasters, wars, rebellions, and the like. But about the time of Alexander's conquest of that area (4th century BC) individual horoscopes began to be cast.

Although the Babylonian system set the pattern for the development of astrology in the west, there were other countries practising their own types of astrology, now forgotten. The pre-Columbian civilisations of Central and South America, for example, had a system of astrology, as is suggested by a pastoral letter written in 1698 by a Catholic bishop referring to astrological practices among the Quiche Indians: 'They believe,' the bishop writes, 'that the birth of men is regulated by the course of the stars and planets; they observe the time of day and the month at which a child is born, and predict the conditions of its life and destiny, both favourable and unfavourable. And the worst of it is that these perverted men have written down their signs and rules so as to deceive the erring and the ignorant.'

The Maya had a set of priest-astronomers, rather like those of Babylonia, who observed the movements of the heavenly bodies from the tops of pyramids. Venus was one of the planets they most revered, and they worked out a calendar of its movements over a 384-year period. They are also believed to have had a zodiac consisting of 13 signs instead of 12. A form of astrology was also practised among the Aztecs. Most of the clues to these systems were, like so much else, swept away by the missionary zeal of the Spanish conquistadors, and little trace of them remains today.

It was from south-eastern Europe and Mesopotamia that the mainstream of astrology flowed. The Babylonian science was taken to Greece by a priest called Berosus who set up an astrological school on the Greek island of Cos. Astrology found a ready audience in Greece, particularly among the Stoics, who already had ideas about celestial forces, and the influence of destiny. Greek mathematics also helped to strengthen astrology.

In all the countries that came under Greek influence, astrology made itself felt. In Egypt, King Ptolemy III was indirectly responsible for the naming of a new constellation. Soon after his marriage he had to go to war in Syria and his wife, Berenice, took a vow that if only he would return safely she would cut off her hair, renowned for its beauty. When she heard that the king was returning she kept her vow, and Ptolemy was furious when he returned home to a hairless wife. In order to abate his anger the priests declared that the hair had mysteriously disappeared during the night and had transformed itself into a new constellation in the sky. Ptolemy must have believed the story, for to this day the constellation of Coma Berenices or 'The Hair of Berenice' can be seen in the sky.

Egypt also gave birth to the man who could be described as the father of astrology – Claudius Ptolemy (no relation to the king). He lived at Alexandria and his two most influential works were the *Almagest* and the *Tetrabiblos*. The former was astronomical, the latter, astrological. The *Tetrabiblos*, which remained a bible of astrology for many centuries, was the most complete manual of the subject yet written. It contained a justification for the belief in planetary influence as well as detailed instructions for interpreting positions in a horoscope. Part of the book deals with 'general' or 'universal' astrology, relating to countries and geographical areas. 'The natives of those countries which lie towards the east,' says Ptolemy, 'excel in courage, acting boldly and openly under all circumstances; for in all their characteristics they are principally conformed to the Sun's nature which is oriental, diurnal, masculine and dexter.' Of the inhabitants of Britain and Germany he states that they 'have a greater share of familiarity with Aries and Mars . . . and are accordingly wilder, bolder and more ferocious.'

One of the ways in which astrology was developed by the Greeks was its use in medicine. In averting diseases and ailments care had to be taken during so-called 'climacteric' years, that is to say, years which were particularly critical in a person's life. These could be calculated from the horoscope. Today the word climacteric is still used to refer to a critical period in a lifetime. There was also built up a complex series of associations between signs and planets on the one hand, and parts of the body and remedies on the other.

In deciding on remedies recourse was often had to the writings of the mythological Egyptian king, Nechepso, who had supposedly received his astrological knowledge from his priest, Petosiris. The story is told of a doctor who had applied Nechepso's remedies to his patient without

success. He was about to declare Nechepso an imposter
when the god Asklepios, patron of medicine, appeared to
him and explained that he had neglected to observe the
proper times and places for picking his medicinal plants.
Hemlock, for example, was produced by the evil influence
of Mars. If picked in Italy it was poison, since Italy was
governed by Scorpio, which is ruled by Mars. In Crete, on
the other hand, hemlock acts as a cure, because the influence of Mars is lessened by that of Sagittarius, the sign
ruling Crete. As for the time when plants should be picked,
it was important to know that when the Sun was in Aries
the virtues of all planets and their subsidiary plants were
increased. Furthermore, one should pick a plant on the
day and hour corresponding to the plant's ruling planet.
For example, hemlock should be picked on a Tuesday, the
day ruled by Mars.

So firmly did astrology take hold that it came to be in-
corporated into other forms of divination. For example,
interpreters of dreams developed the theory that dreams
were true under certain signs of the zodiac and false under
others. Palmists gave astrological names to the different
parts of the hand.

From Greece, astrology passed on to Rome, where it
gathered an even larger following as well as stirring up
some strong opposition. Cato, for example, forbade the
overseer of his estate to consult 'Chaldeans' – the term used
at that time to refer to anyone who practised astrology;
and the poet Juvenal warned his readers to 'avoid meeting
with a lady who is always casting up her ephemerides, who
is so good an astrologer that she has ceased to consult and
is already beginning to be consulted; such a one on the
inspection of the stars will refuse to accompany her husband to the army or to his native land.'

Some of the emperors feared the influence of astrology,
and under Augustus, in 33 BC, all astrologers and magicians were expelled from Rome. This action can have had
little permanent effect, for astrology continued to in-

fluence the Roman world. Augustus's motives were probably political, for he himself was a believer in astrology to the extent that he had a coin struck bearing the symbol of his sign, Capricorn.

Many Roman writers dealt with astrology in their works. The elder Pliny discussed it in his *Natural History*, which included a part dealing with medicinal herbs and their planetary correspondences. Manilius devoted a long poem to astrology, and Horace in one of his poems asked himself if he was born under Libra, Scorpio, or Capricorn.

Roman religion and theories of the afterlife were much influenced by astrology; one of the beliefs commonest at the time was that when great men died they were transported to the sky where they lived forever as constellations. Hercules, Perseus, Castor, and Pollux were all heroes who had been given this privilege. According to another theory the soul was encumbered with planetary qualities, gathered as it descended to be born on earth. After death it had to pass back up through the spheres of the planets casting off these encumbrances like onion skins and reaching the outermost heaven in its original pure state.

One of the practices that became widespread during the Roman period was horary astrology, that is to say the use of astrology to answer questions relating to a specific event rather than to a person's birth chart. In the year AD 479, for example, an astrologer named Palchus was asked what had happened to a ship that had disappeared on a voyage between Alexandria in Egypt and Smyrna in Asia Minor. His answer was that the ship 'had encountered a violent storm, but had escaped inasmuch as Venus and the Moon were beheld by Jupiter'. The ship's company, he said, would have passed from one ship to another because the ascendant was in a double sign. It is not recorded whether this interpretation was correct.

Another use of astrology was in 'elections', a term referring to advice given by astrologers on the most auspicious time for beginning an undertaking. An account of a bad piece of such advice being given is related by Palchus, who tells the story of a man named Leontios who tried to establish himself as emperor in opposition to the existing emperor Zeno who ruled from Constantinople. 'Those who made the election much fancied the rising of the Sun, Jupiter and Mars, with Mercury succedent to them, and the good aspects of the Moon to Saturn and Jupiter. But they did not pay attention to the fact that Mercury, ruler of the day and of the next evening hour, was in evil case.' The result was that Leontios and his lieutenant Illus were defeated by the emperor's armies and forced to flee. Putting the blame on the astrologer they cut off his head and hung the body from the battlements of their castle.

Astrology continued to flourish in Rome even after Christianity had become the official religion of the empire. Indeed, certain early Christian fathers, such as Synesius, were often open supporters of astrology. But a major offensive against it was launched by St Augustine (AD 354–430) who declared that astrology was false, but that evil demons sometimes made predictions come true in order to lead men astray. The opposition of Augustine and his supporters carried the day, and astrology entered a period of eclipse which continued until well into the middle ages.

In the Arab world, however, astrology was kept very much alive. Although the Muslim religion did not officially encourage astrology it was more tolerant towards it than the Christian church, and throughout the Muslim world there were centres of learning where astrology was studied and practised. The most influential of the Arab astrologers was probably Albumasar, who practised at Baghdad and died in about AD 886. Many of his works, including his widely read *Introduction to Astronomy*, were translated into Latin.

It was the works of Arab astrologers like Albumasar which, percolating through to the Christian world, caused the revival of astrology in Europe. Its return to respectability was helped by the Church's enthusiasm for Aristotle, many of whose theories had an astrological colouring. Astrology also found an ally in Thomas Aquinas whose writings on the subject helped to mitigate the Church's opposition. Much astrological knowledge emanated from the Jewish and Arab schools in Muslim Spain. There were also centres in other countries. Italy had chairs of astrology at Bologna, Padua, and Milan. Astrology also began to creep into literature again. Dante's *Divine Comedy*, for example, contains much astrological symbolism.

By the time of the Renaissance astrology was firmly entrenched in European thought and practice. The presence of an astrologer at the court of a great potentate was a common phenomenon, and the practice of casting horoscopes for a child's birth was very widespread among all classes. Astrology still had its attackers, like the Italian philosopher Pico della Mirandola, who gave instances of false predictions concerning members of his family. His brother-in-law, for example, had died during the course of a year which the astrologers had promised would be completely free of misfortune. But such attacks only show how widespread was the preoccupation with astrology at that time.

This preoccupation continued even after Copernicus, Galileo, and Kepler had turned their scientific minds on the heavens and made discoveries which upset many of the old astrological theories. Copernicus had rediscovered the fact that the Earth moves round the Sun, and not vice versa, but still the astrologers believed in their Earth-centred universe. Poets, philosophers, and theologians continued to be inspired by the thought that human destiny was reflected in the movements of the celestial bodies.

Gradually, however, as the 'Age of Enlightenment' dawned the attitude towards astrology began to change. During the sceptical 18th century it went into a decline. By then few people considered it even worth refuting. Few astrological writings of any note were produced during the 18th century, and things were made very difficult for the astrologers. In addition to being scorned by the intelligentsia they were outlawed by the Vagrancy Act of 1736.

But astrology survived this lean period and, after a century or so of eclipse, began to come back into vogue. By the beginning of the 19th century a whole new literate public had emerged and a new type of astrologer was beginning to appear. The era of mass astrology was on its way.

8

The Growth of Mass Astrology

When the Moon is in the Seventh House
And Jupiter aligns with Mars
Then peace will guide the planets
And love will steer the stars.

from *Aquarius*, song in the musical, *Hair*.

THE fact that astrology has now crept into popular songs is one of the indications that it is 'sinking into the racial unconscious', to quote the phrase used by a leading British astrologer recently interviewed in the press. This state of affairs is largely due to the propagation of astrology through the star columns in the national press. However much the more intellectual astrologer may look down on newspaper astrology there is no doubt that it has had a tremendous influence and has turned the names of the signs of zodiac into practically household words.

The forerunners of the newspaper astrologers of today were the popular almanac writers of the 17th century, men like William Lilly, John Gadbury, George Wharton, and John Partridge. Lilly became famous for his prediction of the Great Fire of London, which was so accurate that he was suspected of having been involved in a plot to cause the fire. He was, however, acquitted after convincing a parliamentary court that his foreknowledge was not due to anything other than his astrological calculations.

The spread of literacy, the growth of the printing industry and an unsettled political climate all helped to create conditions which favoured the flourishing of predictive writers. In Britain, printing and publishing were more highly developed than anywhere else in Europe, and it was here that astrology prospered most. The number of astrological books and almanacs issued in the 16th century in Britain exceeded the total output for the whole of the rest of Europe at that time.

The Stationers' Company, an association for members of the various branches of the book trade, had a monopoly of the publishing of almanacs and was responsible for such publications as John Partridge's *Merlinus Liberatus*, Henry Season's *Speculum Anni*, and Francis Moore's *Vox Stellarum*. Moore's publication was the most successful, and it still continues today under the name of *Old Moore's Almanac*.

These almanacs kept interest in astrology alive throughout the sceptical 18th century, and by the early 19th century a revival of interest in astrology had begun. In 1803 Moore's publication had a print order of 393,750 copies. In the 1820s an important event occurred in the history of astrology with the appearance of Robert Cross Smith who, in 1824, took over the editorship of a magazine called *The Straggling Astrologer*. Although this magazine ran only for a few issues it represents an interesting development, for it was the first magazine to carry a regular *weekly* astrological predictive feature, giving readers prognostications about love, marriage, business, travel, and so on, just like the astrological columns of today.

When the *Straggling Astrologer* folded up, Smith was put in charge of a new venture called the *Prophetic Messenger*, which he wrote under the pseudonym of Raphael. In this publication he introduced forecasts for every day of the year, something he had not done before. After Smith's death in 1832 the magazine continued under a succession of different Raphaels, and is still published today under the title of *Raphael's Almanac, Prophetic Messenger and Weather Guide*.

By the time the first Raphael died another major astrological publicist had appeared on the scene. This was R. J. Morrison, who wrote under the name of Zadkiel. He was a much more educated man than Smith and made serious attempts to defend astrology on scientific grounds. He was particularly interested in its use in weather forecasting. In 1844 he founded the British Association for the Advancement of Astral and Other Sciences, the first association of its kind; though it was short-lived it was to serve as the example for many subsequent astrological associations in the 20th century. Morrison's publication *Zadkiel's Almanac* gained a wide circulation and continued to be published for many years after his death.

By the end of the 19th century the craze for astrology, until then a mainly British preoccupation, had spread to the continent, and it was not long before it became a widely popular subject of discussion.

But not until the 1930s was astrology taken up by the national press. The first national newspaper astrologer was R. H. Naylor who began contributing to the *Sunday Express* in August 1930. He soon gained wide fame for his startling predictions. J. R. Gordon, editor at the time, described two of these predictions in a foreword to one of Naylor's books:

The first time was in the early hours of that terrible Sunday morning when the R101 pitched to the earth in flames, destroying all but a handful of her crew. I raced by car through the night to the *Sunday Express,* turned the pages of a copy of the newspaper wet from the printing presses, and there in the middle of Mr Naylor's weekly article set by some strange freak of Fate, boldly in black type, was a prophecy of the R101 disaster.

The second occasion was equally fantastic. One Saturday afternoon Mr Naylor walked into my office. Lord Castlerosse was sitting at my side. 'Can I add something to my article?' said Naylor. 'There is going to be an earthquake.'

'I'm sorry,' I said, 'but you are too late.'

Twelve hours later the telephone at my bedside rang, and a voice from the *Sunday Express* office described briefly and vividly to me the earthquake that an hour before had rocked half England.

Along with the growth in newspaper astrology there has been a corresponding growth in the number of people who go to astrologers for advice. In America, particularly, the increase has been remarkable. According to a recent estimate there are about 10,000 full-time and 175,000 part-time astrologers in the United States. A number of companies are now making use of computers to cast and interpret horoscopes. One American company has programmed a computer to turn out a 10,000-word horoscope reading in two minutes. Computerised astrology is also spreading rapidly in Europe. Advertisers too now realise the potential of astrology. There are zodiac perfumes, zodiac shoes and even zodiac cocktails.

All this is, of course, anathema to the more serious followers of astrology who are also growing in number. Many of them would like to get rid of the term astrology altogether and substitute something with less frivolous connotations. In Germany this has already come about to some extent, and the term 'cosmobiology' is a widely used alternative. The 'serious' astrological fraternity are represented by such bodies as the Astrological Association and the Astrological Lodge of the Theosophical Society. Their members are an interesting cross-section from many different professions – doctors, engineers, lawyers; and they cut across all age groups. Paradoxically, the most serious and intelligent exponents of astrology are very rarely full-time professional astrologers. In fact to be a professional astrologer is to invite suspicion and even distrust from the non-professionals. This is a curious situation, which is surely unique to astrology. It has come about because for the last 500 years astrology has been denied any official recognition as a profession and therefore astrologers have operated free of any controls or restrictions such as those enforced in the medical profession. Furthermore, anyone with a minimum of knowledge can fairly easily give the impression of being a practised astrologer. Hence the practice is wide open to confidence tricksters. This has been the case for so long that anyone who actually makes money out of astrology is immediately suspect. The Astrological Association and other bodies award diplomas and certificates which demand that the candidates undergo a long course of instruction and sit an examination occupying many hours. They hope in this way to give astrology a professional status.

Many of the serious exponents of astrology feel that it has tremendous potentialities in the fields of psychology, criminology, medical diagnosis, vocational guidance and other related fields. Astrologers with these leanings regard Carl Jung as their apostle.

Jung postulated that all forms of divination were based on what he called 'synchronicity'. This he defined as something which made events related to one another without there being any causal connection. As an example, Jung quotes one of his own experiences: 'A young woman I was treating had, at a critical moment, a dream in which she was given a golden scarab. While she was telling me this dream I sat with my back to the closed window. Suddenly I heard a flying insect knocking against the window pane from outside. I opened the window and caught the creature in the air as it flew in. It was the nearest analogy to a golden scarab that one finds in our latitude, a scarabaeid beetle.' Obviously the woman's dream could not have caused the appearance of the beetle. On the other hand Jung felt that such an incident was more than a *mere* coincidence. It was a *meaningful* coincidence. The same thing, he claimed, was to be found in the case of predictive dreams, long runs in gambling, ESP, and other such phenomena.

Looking round for a way of putting this to the test,

Jung hit on astrology. He took as the basis of his experiment the astrological belief that marriage was strongly indicated by the conjunction of one partner's Sun with the other's Moon, or alternatively by the conjunction of the two Moons. Jung set to work and analysed the horoscopes of 400 married couples. With the help of a statistician he computed the results and found that the incidence of the two vital conjunctions was no greater than chance would allow. But in listing all the important aspects in the horoscopes he found that the Sun-Moon conjunctions came top of the list in frequency. This he believed proved his point: that the astrological correspondences were not causal (otherwise this would have shown in the statistics), but were based on synchronicity, or meaningful coincidence.

Concluding his study entitled *Synchronicity: An Acausal Connecting Principle*, Jung points out: 'Though the West has done everything possible to discard this antiquated hypothesis [synchronicity], it has not quite succeeded. Certain mantic procedures seem to have died out, but astrology, which in our own day has attained an eminence never known before, remains very much alive. Nor has the determination of the scientific epoch been able to extinguish altogether the persuasive power of the synchronicity principle. For in the last resort it is not so much a question of superstition as of a truth which remained hidden for so long only because it had less to do with the physical side of events than with their psychic aspects.'

Jung's whole sympathetic approach to the symbolism of astrology, alchemy, and other ancient systems helped to pioneer a new respect among psychologists for modes of thought which had not long before been regarded with contempt. Today there are many psychologists, personnel managers, probation officers, and others concerned with character typology who are finding astrology a way of helping them to understand the people with whom they deal.

These developments show the interesting way in which

astrology has evolved over the centuries. It started as the prerogative of priests and seers; later it became a popular preoccupation, scorned by the educated; now it is once again seeping upwards from its mass following and is being taken seriously by intellectuals.

9

A New Science of the Stars?

How do you know that the pilgrim track
Along the belting zodiac
Swept by the sun in his seeming rounds
Is traced by now to the Fishes' bounds
And into the Ram, when weeks of cloud
Have wrapt the sky in a clammy shroud,
And never as yet a tinct of spring
Has shown in the Earth's apparelling:
   O vespering bird, how do you know,
   How do you know?

Thomas Hardy, from *Satires of Circumstance*

CAN astrology and science ever come together again, or is their divorce to be permanent? The esoteric astrologer would say that science and astrology are irreconcilable because astrology has to do with symbols, not facts. The scientist would also say that they are irreconcilable because the word astrology is to him synonymous with nonsensical superstition. But supposing we were to put the question another way and ask: 'will we ever have scientifically-based knowledge about the influence of the heavenly bodies such that through this knowledge we can predict certain events and explain certain phenomena in human beings?' The answer to this question would be yes. Already we can see the beginnings of a new science of the stars that in many ways more closely resembles astrology than astronomy.

Astronomers have recently been investigating the way gravity works in the solar system as a whole; and they have come up with some very interesting discoveries. One important fact that has emerged is that the gravitational centre around which the planets revolve does not always coincide with the centre of the Sun. What in fact happens is that the Sun, and the planets, orbit around a common centre of gravity. This centre does not remain stationary, but shifts its position as it is pulled this way and that by the gravitational force of the planets.

Because the Sun is thousands of times bigger than any other body in the solar system the centre of gravity is always in or around the Sun, but never in the same position for long. It is sometimes near the centre, sometimes half way to the surface, sometimes thousands of miles beyond the surface.

These movements in the centre of gravity have tremendously far-reaching effects on the solar system, causing solar flares and disturbances of the Sun's all-embracing magnetic field. The disturbances permeate to the upper layers of the earth's atmosphere and affect the weather and other conditions on earth.

Now what is significant about all this for the astrologer is that different types of magnetic disturbance are brought about by different planetary groupings. In the early part of 1962 the centre of gravity of the solar system was drawn farther out from the Sun than ever before by the combined force of Mercury, Venus, Mars, Jupiter, and Saturn, which were all lined up on one side of the Sun. Even the tiny planet Mercury can exercise a significant influence on the position of the centre because of the planet's proximity to the Sun. It is a well-known law that the gravitational force of any body diminishes by the square of its distance from the body on which the force is operating. Thus, although Mercury is a tiny fraction of the size of Jupiter, it often exercises a far greater gravitational force than Jupiter, because it is much closer to the Sun.

An article on this subject in *Analog*, December 1968, states that: 'Of all the planets, fast-moving Mercury is responsible for the most unusual kinds of weather. It helps to whipsaw solar plasma by exerting its influence on a regular rhythm of 88-day intervals. The Moon has been suspected of being the final triggering force for "focusing" certain kinds of radiation from the Sun. Medieval astrologers referred to it as "the lens".'

But it is not only the planets that affect weather conditions on earth. Not long ago the United States Naval Observatory announced that it had observed that barometric pressure fluctuated in phase with the positions of distant stars. At the same time Dr Harry B. Marvis, a Naval Observatory astronomer, told the American Institute of Physics that, 'In accurate weather forecasting of the future, the contributions of the stars to barometric changes will have to be considered.'

Already astronomical methods are used in weather forecasting. For example, a company called Electro-Weather, a tornado forecasting service in Kansas City, finds that by calculating the times of eclipses and planetary conjunctions and oppositions it can predict when tornadoes will take place.

Other research organisations in the United States have found that earthquakes can be related to planetary interactions. Earthquakes are always preceded by disturbances in the earth's magnetic field, caused by planetary movements. For example, fourteen hours before the earthquake at Anchorage, Alaska, in March 1964, electrical earth current readings from Kansas indicated a strong disturbance in the Anchorage area.

A proper understanding of the types of planetary configuration causing earthquakes could enable the inhabitants of a threatened area to abandon it before the earthquake struck.

The planets not only influence weather and earthquakes. They also affect earthly conditions in much subtler ways. For example, it has been shown that the movements of the Moon affect the mental state of human beings. Recently a three-year study was completed at Philadelphia, co-sponsored by the American Institute of Medical Climatology, a group of hospitals and mental institutions, the fire and police departments, and several large industrial corporations. The conclusion of the study was that celestial occurrences such as solar and lunar eclipses affect such factors as barometric pressure, moisture level, and electro-magnetic imbalances in the atmosphere; these, in turn, have a demonstrable effect on the way people feel, think and behave.

One of the people who have studied this subject intensively is Dr Robert O. Becker of Syracuse University, in New York State. He and his team discovered that both physical and mental diseases could be related to solar disturbances. He proved his theory by successfully predicting the times of the largest number of admissions to New York mental hospitals. Dr Becker said:

Every organism demonstrates cycles of biological and mental-emotional activity closely linked to geomagnetic force-field patterns and more complex force-field interrelations, both planetary and solar-terrestrial in scope. Human behaviour is influenced through the direct current control system of the brain by the terrestrial magnetic field, solar and planetary conditions, and both high and low energy cosmic radiation.

So it looks as though the old connection between the Moon and lunacy (from the Latin word meaning moon) has something in it after all.

Another interesting effect of the Moon has been discovered by two Florida doctors, Carl S. McLemore and Edson Andrews, who examined the periods of excessive bleeding in certain of their patients particularly prone to this complaint. Their findings, reported in the *Journal of the Florida Medical Association*, were that haemorrhaging reached a peak each month at the time when the Moon was in opposition to the Sun, and reached its lowest level at the New Moon.

These discoveries point to the fact that life on earth is strongly affected by cosmic rhythms, of which the solar and lunar cycles are the most obvious. Probably the world's greatest authority on the biological effects of these cycles is Professor Frank A. Brown of the Department of Biological Sciences at Northwestern University, Illinois. During the course of studying the habits of a wide variety of creatures, from crabs to hamsters, Professor Brown observed that every living thing responds to a number of complex rhythms.

These rhythms, Brown maintains, can be divided into two different categories: (a) environmental rhythms which are dependent on such factors as light, temperature, and feeding schedule and which can be changed; and (b) rhythms which are dependent on cosmic cycles, and which are very difficult to interfere with.

The most familiar rhythm to us is the 24-hour solar-day rhythm of sleeping and waking; but lunar rhythms are also important. The monthly lunar rhythm is tied to the reproductive cycle. As Brown points out in a paper entitled *Bioastronautics*: 'The vast majority of all the individuals in any given species have their rhythms synchronised so that the climax of the reproductive processes occurs in all, at closely the same time in any particular region. . . . There are good reasons to believe that the monthly rhythms of the human female . . . is basically the same phenomenon.'

Lunar-day rhythms are also observable, particularly in creatures of the sea-shore. Oysters and barnacles, for example, are timed to have most activity at flood tide, while shore birds and fiddler crabs have their peak at low tide. Research has shown that if you take a crab away from the beach and place it in a laboratory, it will continue to gear its pattern of activity to the *actual* variations of the tide, however far it is from the sea.

These phenomena, says Brown, cannot be explained by any internal timing mechanism in the animal. This has been proved by animals placed in hermetically sealed containers, in constant conditions, who still react to cyclical changes outside, however much these may be distorted by weather conditions.

Brown quotes the experiment carried out by his colleague, Franklin Barnwell, who observed the behaviour of snails sealed in similar conditions and found that certain changes in the snails tied in with changes in the earth's magnetic field. 'This suggested that some pervasive force, probably of solar origin . . . was influencing . . . organisms.'

Reading passages like that one is struck by the way in which the language of modern science often has echoes of a more mystical past. Could this 'pervasive force' that Brown speaks of be the same force that astrologers have believed in for centuries? Perhaps the 1st-century Alexandrian astronomer-astrologer, Ptolemy, was aware of this force. He spoke of 'a certain power derived from aetherial nature' which pervaded the entire atmosphere and which he called the 'Ambient'. This, he believed, was the vehicle by which celestial forces are transmitted.

The scientist would object that Ptolemy's conclusion had been arrived at by a completely unscientific process and that, although his ambient theory might have a grain of truth in it, there was certainly no logical basis for the rest of his astrological theory with its very precise interpretations of planetary movements.

To this the astrologer might reply that the mysteries of today are the science of tomorrow. Hypnotism is a case in point. When the Austrian doctor, Mesmer, began practising his hypnotic system of curing in the 18th century his theories were scorned by the medical authorities. Yet today it is recognised by scientists that there is a hypnotic effect and that it has a use in medicine.

So perhaps one day, out of all these discoveries, there

will emerge a new science of cosmic influences. It may not coincide exactly with the old astrological tradition, but in essence it would be a form of astrology.

So far I have discussed only general planetary influences – on weather, earthquakes, and so on. But what about planetary influences at the moment of a person's birth? Is there any scientific proof that the birth positions are significant? The man who has done most research on this is the French statistician, Michel Gauquelin. He began by casting the horoscopes of 25,000 men from all over Europe, each of whom distinguished himself in some profession. Gauquelin then examined the horoscopes to see if certain planets were more prominent in the case of certain professions. He came up with some surprising results. For example he found that people with Mars prominent tended to become doctors, sportsmen, or army officers. Actors and politicians, on the other hand, showed Jupiter prominent.

In order to explain these phenomena without recourse to traditional astrology, Gauquelin developed a theory of 'planetary heredity'. This postulated that children tend to be born under the same cosmic conditions as their parents, which is born out, Gauquelin found, by the fact that horoscopes of parents and children show similarity in a significant number of cases. According to Gauquelin, the mechanism by which this 'planetary heredity' works comes into action as birth approaches. Certain planetary forces accelerate or decelerate labour so as to make the cosmic pattern of the child synchronise with that of the parents.

These various researches may not be grist to the mill of traditional astrology, but they do show that serious scientists are becoming increasingly interested in the whole question of cosmic influence. We may yet see the development of a new science that is half way between astrology and astronomy.

IO

Astrology and Magic

Whatever the stars can do we can do ourselves.
Franz Hartmann, *Paracelsus.*

MAGICIANS, from those of antiquity to those of the 20th century like Aleister Crowley, have frequently made use of astrology. The magician believes that his spells and incantations are rendered much more powerful if he invokes the aid of the heavenly bodies and carries out his operations when the planetary configurations are favourable.

The main bearers of the western magical tradition were the Jews – or rather a certain movement within the Jewish religion. The Jews probably learned their astrology from the Babylonians, and in the Old Testament there are many references to the stars and planets. For example, in the story of Joseph, in Genesis 37, 9, Joseph tells his brothers of a dream in which '. . . behold the sun and the moon and the eleven stars made obeisance to me'. The 'eleven stars' probably refer to the eleven-signed zodiac used at one time in Babylonia. In Judges V, 20, we read: 'They fought from heaven; the stars in their course fought against Sisera.' And Amos's followers are advised to: 'Seek him that maketh the seven stars in Orion and turneth the shadow of death into the morning.' The symbolism of the Jewish religion also points to astrology; the seven-branched candlestick reflects the seven planets, and the twelve tribes of Israel have been associated with the twelve signs of the zodiac.

The more mystically-minded Jews recorded their thought in a series of medieval writings which have become known as the Cabala; these contain a great deal of astrological symbolism. The Jewish magician believed in a hierarchy of angels and demons, headed by the seven archangels who were believed to govern the seven traditional planets. Raphael governed the Sun; Gabriel, the Moon; Michael, Mercury; Haniel, Venus; Chamael, Mars; Zadkiel, Jupiter; and Zaphkiel, Saturn.

According to a later tradition, enshrined in the book of *Arb 'at' al*, the firmament and the kingdom of heaven is divided into 196 provinces ruled over by seven supreme angels, each of whom was served by a horde of subordinate officials and servants.

Aratron, the first angel, was identified with Saturn. He ruled over 49 provinces. He could transmute metals and change beasts or vegetables into stones. He ruled 49 kings, 42 princes, 35 satraps, 28 dukes, 21 servants, 14 councillors and 7 envoys, and he commanded 36,000 legions of spirits, each legion containing 490 members. The second angel was Bethor, identified with Jupiter. He ruled over 42 provinces and commanded a smaller, though still impressive array of etherial forces. The other angels were: Phalag, Mars; Och, Sun; Hagith, Venus; Ophiel, Mercury; and Phul, Moon.

The cabalistic magician believed that these beings exercised a powerful influence on the world through the planets, and the first thing he had to learn was which times were governed by which planet, so that he could carry out his rituals under the appropriate influence.

In the system used by the magician each of the seven days of the week is ruled by a planet as follows:

Sunday	Sun
Monday	Moon
Tuesday	Mars
Wednesday	Mercury
Thursday	Jupiter
Friday	Venus
Saturday	Saturn

Certain Jews suggested that Friday was the best day for weddings because of its connection with Venus.

Besides the connection with the days of the week there is also a connection in cabalism between the letters of the Hebrew alphabet and the signs and planets. The seven so-called 'double' letters of the alphabet correspond to the seven planets, while the twelve 'single' letters correspond to the signs of the zodiac. The remaining three are known as the 'mother' letters.

The system also relates each of the planets to a different organ of perception: the Moon is connected with the right eye, Mars with the right ear, the Sun with the right nostril, Venus with the left eye, Mercury with the left ear, Saturn with the left nostril, and Jupiter with the mouth.

Each of the planets had a traditional colour and was connected with a particular metal, as the following table shows.

Planet	Metal	Colour
Sun	Gold	Gold
Moon	Silver	Silver
Mercury	Mercury	Mixed colours
Venus	Copper	Green
Mars	Iron	Red
Jupiter	Tin	Blue
Saturn	Lead	Black

The way in which the planets were connected with the hours of the day was slightly less straightforward. The hours were counted from sunrise on. The first hour after sunrise was governed by the planet ruling the day in question, and the remaining hours were governed by each of the planets in turn, following this order: Sun, Venus, Mercury, Moon, Saturn, Jupiter, Mars.

If you wanted to perform some feat by magical means it was important to choose the appropriate day and/or hour. A magical textbook called the *Key of Solomon the King* advises the reader on which hours to choose for different types of operation. The planetary days and hours and the activities they favour can be summarised as follows:

Sun

Obtaining wealth, gaining favour of princes, making friends.

Moon

Voyages, messages, love.

Mercury

Business, divination, wonders, apparitions,

Venus

Making friends, love, travel.

Mars

Summoning souls from Hades.

Jupiter

Obtaining honours, acquiring riches, preserving health.

Saturn

Causing good or ill fortune to business, possessions, goods acquiring learning; sowing destruction, death and discord.

Most of the spells given in the magical textbooks such as the *Key of Solomon* begin with an instruction about choosing the right planetary influence. For example a spell for making oneself invisible begins: 'Make a small image of yellow wax, in the form of a man, in the month of January and in the day and hour of Saturn.' Another for making a magic carpet begins: 'Make a carpet of white and new wool, and when the Moon shall be at her full, in the sign of Capricorn and in the hour of the Sun, thou shalt go into the country . . . and shall spread out the carpet so that one of its points shall be towards the east, and another towards the west.' The position of the Moon is considered particularly important for magical operations, and the *Key of Solomon* advises: 'At all times of practising and putting into execution Magical Arts, the Moon should be increasing in light, and in an equal number of degrees with the Sun; and it is much better from the first quarter of the Opposition, and the Moon should be in a fiery sign, and notably in that of the Ram or of the Lion.'

An important aid for the magician in enlisting the help of the planetary forces was the use of talismans, that is symbols written or engraved on parchment, wood, metal or stone. Often the talisman for a particular planet was engraved on a piece of the appropriate metal, for example, tin for Jupiter. If the talisman was written on parchment then the planetary colour would be used. Rings were also used as a form of talisman and were recommended to be made in the following materials.

Sun
: diamond or topaz set in gold

Moon
: pearl, crystal, or quartz set in silver

Mercury
: opal or agate set in mercury

Venus
: emerald or turquoise set in copper

Mars
: ruby or any red stone set in iron

Jupiter

>sapphire, amethyst, or cornelian set in tin

Saturn

>onyx or sapphire set in lead

The Key to Solomon refers to talismans as 'medals' or 'pentacles' and gives instructions for making seven different pentacles for each planet, every one of which has a different purpose. For the seventh pentacle of Mars, the *Key* says: 'Write thou this upon virgin parchment or paper with the blood of a bat, in the day and hour of Mars; and uncover it within the Circle, invoking the Demons whose names are therein written: and thou shalt immediately see hail and tempest.'

The sixth pentacle of Mars had a different purpose. 'It hath so great virtue that being armed therewith, if thou art attacked by any one thou shalt neither be injured nor wounded when thou fightest with him, and his own weapons shall turn against him.' The fifth pentacle of Mars has a different purpose again, enabling the magician to command the obedience of demons.

Sometimes these talismans were engraved with complex hieroglyphs and Hebrew letters. Another type of inscription found on talismans was a series of numbers known as a 'magical square'. There were seven of these squares, one for each of the planets. Examples are shown in Figure 5.

4	9	2
3	5	7
8	1	6

SATURN

4	14	15	1
9	7	6	12
5	11	10	8
16	2	3	13

JUPITER

11	24	7	20	3
4	12	25	8	16
17	5	13	21	9
10	18	1	14	22
23	6	19	2	15

MARS

Figure 5

These sets of numbers had various properties. For example, any row or column in the square of Saturn adds up to fifteen, which is the numerical equivalent of the Hebrew letters corresponding to YH, the shortened form of YHVH, the tetragrammaton or name of God (pronounced 'Yaweh'). The total of the three columns adds up to forty-five, the number of the planets governing spirit.

In the case of the Jupiter square, a row or column adds up to thirty-four, the numerical equivalent of the word for tin, which is the metal ruled by Jupiter. The total of numbers adds up to 136, again the number of the spirit or demon ruling the planet.

A magical textbook called the *Grimorium Verum* gives an interesting love spell which makes use of the planetary forces. The magician is instructed to begin by preparing a talisman drawn on virgin parchment and consisting of two concentric circles surmounted by a cross. On the western arm of the cross is drawn the symbol of the Sun, on the eastern arm that of the Moon, and on the northern arm a star. He writes the name of the object of his desire in the inner circle and on the other side of the parchment he writes the names Melchidael and Bereschas. At eleven o'clock at night he goes out and puts the parchment on the ground with the woman's name facing downwards. He then places his right foot on the parchment and his left knee on the ground. In his right hand he holds a lighted candle of white wax, large enough to burn for an hour. Then he focuses his attention on the highest star in the sky and recites the following incantation.

I salute and conjure you, O beautiful Moon, O beautiful Star, O brilliant light which I hold in my hand. By the air that I breathe, by the breath within me, by the earth which I touch, I conjure you. By the names of the spirit princes living in you; by the ineffable name ON which created all things; by you, O resplendent Angel Gabriel, with the planet Mercury, Michael and Melchidael. I conjure you by all the Holy Names of God, that you send down power to obsess, torment and harrass the body, the soul and the five senses of N., she whose name is written here below, so that she shall come to me and submit to my desires, liking no one in the world, and especially thus N., for as long as she shall be indifferent to me. So shall she endure not, so shall she be obsessed, so suffer, so be tormented. Go then, quickly. Go Melchidael, Bereschas, Zazel, Firiel, Malcha, and all those who are with you. I conjure you by the Great Living God to obey my will and I, N., promise to satisfy you.

This formula is repeated three times, after which the magician burns the parchment with the candle. Next day he puts the ashes in his left shoe where he keeps them until the woman comes to him.

A recent figure who dabbled in astrological magic was the writer Frederick Rolfe, Baron Corvo, whose novels contain many references to astrology. His biographer, A. J. A. Symons, in *The Quest for Corvo*, quotes a letter from Vyvyan Holland describing the interest shown in Rolfe's astrological dabblings by the latter's friend, Father R. H. Benson.

At that time Father Benson was deeply absorbed in all questions concerning magic, necromancy and spiritualism, and spent a good deal of time in reviewing books on these subjects. He had been deeply impressed with Rolfe's casting of horoscopes. According to Benson, if Rolfe knew the exact place, and the time to the minute, of anyone's birth, he could lay down a scheme for the conduct of his life, in such matters as when it would be wise to go on a journey, or invest money. Father Benson admitted that he himself had paid a good deal of attention to the rules laid down for himself in his own horoscope. He said that Rolfe had evidently devoted a vast amount of time to the study of the stars, had found a number of very obscure books on the subject, including one quite unknown book by Albertus Magnus, and that he probably knew more about astrology than any living man.

The most interesting story, by far, that Father Benson told me was of an experiment in 'White Magic' which he had carried out at Rolfe's request. Rolfe wrote to him one day in a state of great excitement and told him that he had discovered, either in his Albertus Magnus book or in some mediaeval manuscript, instructions as to how to bring about a certain event. He would not, at that juncture, reveal what the event was, but he implored Father Benson to make the experiment.

The account goes on to state that Father Benson followed the complex rules of the magical operation, observing the times specified by Rolfe. Holland continued: 'At the end of the period stated, Father Benson told me that he distinctly saw a white figure whose features were quite indistinguishable, mounted on a horse, ride slowly into the middle of the room and there halt for about half a minute, after which it slowly faded away.'

Another modern magician, Aleister Crowley, used astrological symbolism in his rituals, and gives instructions in his *Magick in Theory and Practice* for the summoning and banishing of planetary spirits. The works of Crowley are now more widely read than ever, and interest in the magical side of astrology will no doubt increase.

11

Separating the Dragons and the Hares: the Chinese Zodiac

The Dragon takes to the cloud at the sight of a Hare.
Old Chinese proverb

MOST countries today follow astrological systems broadly similar to the one I have described. The exception is China where a completely different system is followed. The animals of the Chinese zodiac do not correspond at all to our symbols. If you asked a Chinaman what his sign was he might reply: Dragon, Tiger, Hare, Snake, or Monkey. And he would not be talking about the month of his birth but the year. In Chinese astrology the years go in cycles of twelve, each year being governed by a different sign. Horoscopes are also cast for day and time of birth, but the year is the crucial factor.

Chinese astrology, like much of Chinese thought, rests on the system of the *Yin* and *Yang*. These are the two basic ingredients of the universe. All forms of matter are the result of the combination of these two elements in different ratios. *Yang* is usually represented by one long line and *Yin* by two short lines. They can be put together in a sort of morse code for the purposes of foretelling the future. There is a famous Chinese manual of divination called the *I Ching* which shows how different permutations of *Yin* and *Yang* can be interpreted. *Yang* is associated with the Sun and is masculine in character; it is positive, bright, active, and full of movement. *Yin*, on the other hand, is linked with the Moon, is negative and feminine and is associated with darkness, rest, and passivity. The Chinese signs of the zodiac, as well as the planets, are classified under *Yin* or *Yang*.

Instead of the four elements of western astrology (Fire, Earth, Air, Water) the Chinese have five elements: Wood, Fire, Earth, Metal, and Water, which are governed respectively by Jupiter, Mars, Saturn, Venus, and Mercury. In the old days it was believed that each Imperial dynasty was governed by a different element from the preceding one. It was thought that when a new dynasty was emerging the gods would display the appropriate signs. For example during the rise of the emperor Huang Ti, large earthworms and ants appeared. When he observed this the emperor remarked: 'This indicates that the element earth is in the ascendant, so our colour must be yellow [the colour of the earth element], and our affairs must be placed under the sign of earth.'

Each planet, in addition to ruling an element, had a *Yin* aspect and a *Yang* aspect. The former signified the planet in its *raw*, natural state; the latter corresponded to the element after it had been refined or modified by man. For example, the *Yin* aspect of Jupiter signified wood in its original state as a tree in the forest; the *Yang* aspect was wood when carved or used as a building material.

In the Chinese astrological system the twelve signs govern both the years of the twelve-year cycle and the twelve double-hours of the day. The system also uses what are called the lunar mansions, which correspond to the days of the lunar month. So the Chinese horoscope is a rather complicated affair. But the most important factor is the year of birth. Here is a list of the signs and the years they govern, taken from 1888.

Rat	1888, 1900, 1912, 1924, 1936, 1948, 1960, 1972, 1984
Ox	1889, 1901, 1913, 1925, 1937, 1949, 1961, 1973, 1985
Tiger	1890, 1902, 1914, 1926, 1938, 1950, 1962, 1974, 1986
Hare	1891, 1903, 1915, 1927, 1939, 1951, 1963, 1975, 1987
Dragon	1892, 1904, 1916, 1928, 1940, 1952,1964, 1976, 1988
Serpent	1893, 1905, 1917, 1929, 1941, 1953, 1965, 1977, 1989
Horse	1894, 1906, 1918, 1930, 1942, 1954, 1966, 1978, 1990
Sheep	1895, 1907, 1919, 1931, 1943, 1955, 1967, 1979, 1991
Monkey	1896, 1908, 1920, 1932, 1944, 1956, 1968, 1980, 1992
Cock	1897, 1909, 1921, 1933, 1945, 1957, 1969, 1981, 1993
Dog	1898, 1910, 1922, 1934, 1946, 1958, 1970, 1982, 1994
Boar	1899, 1911, 1923, 1935, 1947, 1959,1971, 1983, 1995

For the benefit of the reader who would like to put the Chinese zodiac to the test, here is a brief run-down of the characteristics of the signs. It is important to remember, by the way, that the Chinese New Year begins in February.

Rat

This is a *Yin* sign. People born under it are gifted with intuition and are able to foresee good and bad luck both for themselves and others. Hence they are fond of prediction. In addition to being able to foresee luck, Rat people also bring luck. Their thoughts are constantly preoccupied with the future. Their opposite is the Horse who plods or gallops about with his thoughts on the present. Their busy minds and imaginations use up a lot of energy, and therefore Rats need a lot of rest. They are recommended to retire to bed early and to rest whenever they feel tired. Some are intrigued by anything secret or hidden. They have a firm sense of loyalty. Those born during the night are bold, adventurous, and outgoing. Those born during the day are more timid and retiring. They are advised not to marry Dogs. Their best marriage partner is the Ox.

Famous Rat people: Shakespeare, Charles, Prince of Wales, Richard Nixon, Vanessa Redgrave, Princess Alexandra.

Ox

Like the Bull of the western zodiac, the Ox is down-to-earth, kind and loving. It is a *Yin* sign, and is associated with the Moon, femininity, and motherhood. Ox men tend to understand women and to need them. Ox people are tender towards their children and make good parents. They are diplomatic and rarely force issues. Often they shirk the limelight, preferring privacy. But they usually command respect from their fellows. Like Rats, they are intuitive and lucky to themselves and others. Women born under this sign are ultra-feminine and are happiest when being fully women; if their feminine side is cramped then sickness follows. Long life is another characteristic of Ox people. Those born in the daytime are in for a rather hard life and have to toil arduously for a living, but those born at night will find that life goes smoothly and easily for them. Ox people, appropriately, like to 'ruminate' and chew over their past experiences. They are fond of leisure. They should not marry horses or sheep, but are very compatible with Rats.

Famous Ox people: Napoleon, Peter Sellers, Charlie Chaplin, Richard Burton.

Tiger

This is a *Yang* sign, reflecting the male qualities of light, warmth, and activity. Tiger people are forceful, intense and sometimes aggressive, even ferocious. Their aggressive qualities are accentuated if they are born after dark. A girl born in the year of the Tiger is feared because she is thought liable to cause her husband's premature death.

For this reason a Tiger girl is usually married to an elderly man because he has less life to risk. On the other hand, the birth of a boy under the Tiger is a happy event, because the ferocity of the Tiger drives away the 'three disasters': thieves, fire, and ghosts. All Tiger people are direct in their dealing with others and always come straight to the point. They are warm-hearted and generous without being extravagant. They should never marry Serpents, as an old Chinese proverb says: 'If the Snake catches a glimpse of the Tiger it is as if it were wounded with a knife.' The best marriage partner for the Tiger is a Boar.

Famous Tiger people: Mary Queen of Scots, General de Gaulle, Sir Ralph Richardson, Princess Anne, Twiggy, Flora Robson.

Hare

A *Yin* sign. Hare people are very sensitive and imaginative. They lead rich and fortunate lives. They are astute and cunning and are gifted with foresight. There is an old Chinese saying that: 'A wily hare has three exits to its burrow, which enables it to avert any tragedy.' Hare people avoid one-way streets, cul-de-sacs, and dead-end jobs. The Hare is warm-hearted beneath the surface, but is often outwardly cold and sometimes shrinks from bodily contact. Hares hate brutality and violence. They are moderate in most things. They should avoid marrying Dragons or Tigers. Their ideal partner is the Dog.

Famous Hare people: Henry James, Sir Alec Douglas-Home, Rudolf Nureyev, Arthur Miller, David Frost, Kenneth Tynan, Georges Simenon.

Dragon

A *Yang* sign, the Dragon signifies rising power. He can change himself into different forms and hence adapts easily to changing conditions. The year of the Dragon is a very auspicious one. Dragons are categorised as big or small. Dragons have wealth, luck, power, long life, and popularity with the opposite sex. Small Dragons have these blessings in smaller measure. All Dragons, big or small, are strong-willed and dislike being ordered about by others. Female Dragons are highly sexed. No Dragon should marry a Hare as the proverb quoted at the beginning of this chapter advises. Monkeys do not make good marriage partners either. The best choice is the Cock.

Famous Dragon people: Edward Heath, Harold Wilson, Paul Getty, Ho Chi-Minh, Nancy Mitford, Angus Ogilvy, Marlene Dietrich, Trevor Howard, Laurence Harvey.

Serpent

This is a *Yang* sign, and the year of the Serpent is auspicious like that of the Dragon. Serpent types are respected but also feared. A boy born in the year of the serpent is fortunate, but a girl has trouble in finding a husband, as female Serpents are thought to be vicious and selfish. However, Serpent women know how to make the best of their difficulties. They are active and forceful. They are not beautiful, but do not allow this to hamper them. Like the Dragon, the Serpent changes frequently to meet changing conditions. Therefore you never quite know where you stand with a Serpent. People born under this sign should avoid marrying Cocks and Tigers. Monkeys are the best choice.

Famous Serpent people: Abraham Lincoln, the Duke of Bedford, the Earl of Longford, Lady Pamela Mountbatten.

Horse

The forceful masculine *Yang* element is very powerful in this sign. Horses are firm, strong, loyal, and reliable. They are full of energy, strength, and speed and lead very full and busy lives, though Horses born at night have a quieter existence than those born during the day. In Chinese legend the Horse is associated with silk, and silk clothes are becoming to people born under this sign. Horse people are tactful and skilled in paying compliments to others; hence they tend to be popular. To quote another old Chinese proverb: 'The white horse will not share a stall with a black cow.' Therefore a Horse should not marry an Ox. The best partner is a Sheep.

Famous Horse people: Genghis Khan, Princess Margaret, the Duke of Windsor, Aristotle Onassis, Harold Pinter, Sean Connery.

Sheep

A *Yin* sign. Sheep make ideal sons and daughters, as they are full of love and respect for their parents. They generally have no desire to depart from the conventions of their family background. They tend to be rather conformist and to lack strong individual impulses. They are proper and decorous in their behaviour, choose their words carefully, and are practical and cautious in their approach to life. They have a chivalrous, even heroic streak in them. They bring luck to other people, and often are associated with people of power and rank. To quote the words of the Chinese writer, Tung Chung-Shu: 'The ram has horns, but he does not use them indiscriminately. . . . When the ram is held in captivity it does not bleat; and when it is slaughtered it does not scream.' Sheep people are good-natured and make good marriage partners, except in the event of their marrying Rats or Oxen with whom they are not compatible. Their ideal marriage partner is the Horse.

Famous Sheep people: Josephine Bonaparte, Margot Fonteyn, Doris Lessing, Iris Murdoch, Sir Laurence Olivier, Lynn Redgrave.

Monkey

This combines the qualities of both *Yin* and *Yang*. Monkey people are awkward customers. They can be selfish, temperamental, petulant, quarrelsome, and irritable. Monkey women are ultra-feminine, but in an active rather than a passive way. Monkey men have a yearning for power and are good at using their wits to attain it. All monkeys are highly intelligent. They are quick, cunning, and crafty. Often they conceal their intelligence until they need it. The best way to deal with Monkey people is to butter them up and appeal to their vanity. They should not marry Boars, nor Dragons. The best choice is the Serpent.

Famous Monkey people: Charles Dickens, the Duke of Norfolk, Elizabeth Taylor, Lyndon Johnson, Mick Jagger, Arnold Wesker, Rex Harrison.

Cock

This is a *Yang* sign. Years of the cock, for example, 1969, are often troubled. Cock people are passionate and are often fond of chasing the opposite sex, though seldom with any depth of feeling or emotion. They are tough, strong-willed, forceful and active. The Cock is regarded as a symbol for warding off evil forces, and for this reason male Cocks are thought to make desirable husbands. Those born during the day are proud and self-confident, but those born at night can be rather more docile. Their best marriage partner is the Dragon. They should avoid marrying Dogs or Serpents.

Famous Cock people: D. H. Lawrence, the Duke of Marlborough, Kwame Nkrumah, Sir Isaac Wolfson, Peter Ustinov, Katherine Hepburn, Harry Secombe, Deborah Kerr.

Dog

People born under the Dog belong to a *Yin* sign. They are alert, quick and observant. 'Watchdog' is an apt description of them, for they are good protectors, both of themselves and others. Those born during the day lead pleasant, easy, and rich lives. Those born at night are destined to toil 'like a dog' for their living. Dog people often appear to their fellows to be officious and interfering, but they usually have the other person's welfare at heart, and their advice should not be ignored. They are unselfish and altruistic. Intuition is one of their strong faculties. Rabbits make good marriage partners; Cocks and Rats do not.

Famous Dog people: Disraeli, Mary Quant, the Earl of Harewood, David Niven, Maggie Smith, Margaret Leighton, Paul Scofield.

Boar

This sign has something of both *Yin* and *Yang*, but more of the former. The Boar is flirtatious, and sometimes even obsessed with sex. Boars are cool and self-possessed by nature. They are reserved and not always frank in their dealings with others. They sometimes spend long periods of apparent inactivity, but they are always alert to danger. They are down-to-earth and practical. They are fond of food and pleasure and tend to live beyond their means. With Monkeys they have a love-hate relationship. The Tiger is their best marriage partner.

Famous Boar people: Oliver Cromwell, Chiang Kai-shek, Barbara Castle, Tennessee Williams, Vladimir Nabokov, Terence Rattigan.

12

Astrology - True or False?

Astrology must be reborn and must perform
again for our modern world.

> Dane Rudhyar, *The Astrology of Personality*

I have described the two ways of looking at astrology: the
scientific and the symbolic. The former believes in reduc-
ing astrology to a set of logically acceptable principles; the
latter places the value on tradition, the set of rules handed
down from antiquity which enable the astrologer to make
predictions by some mysterious psychic means, unknown
to science. In my opinion these two approaches are irreconcilable. I believe that both are valid in their own way,
but that the scientific will eventually dominate. I say this
not to denigrate the symbolic approach. On the contrary;
it was the symbolic approach that paved the way for the
scientific. If it had not been for the astrologer-priests of
Babylon there would have been no Copernicus, no Galileo,
and no Jodrell Bank telescope. And this is the way it is
with all knowledge. Intuition and magic lead the way by
sketching the broad outlines of the picture, then swiftly
move on to some other field leaving their slower and more
painstaking handmaiden, science, to fill in the details.
Once the details have been filled in there is no need for
magic to return. What will happen with astrology is that
a new science of the stars, such as I described in Chapter 9

will develop and the traditional astrologers will seek other
worlds to explore.

Many people will disagree with what I have just said.
More than one traditional astrologer would claim that his
beliefs have already been scientifically proved. So in order
to back up what I have said, let me restate the scientific
case against astrology.

In my opinion the crucial argument against traditional
astrology centres on the precession of the equinoxes, which
I explained in Chapter 2. To sum up again: the signs of
the zodiac no longer coincide with the months with which
they are associated. Because of the precession of the
equinoxes, the Sun no longer rises in Aries in April, but
in Pisces. Therefore when as astrologer talks about an
Arian person he is in fact talking about a Piscean – that is
unless he believes that the signs are not related to the constellations at all, but are only tied to months of the year.
There is a strong movement among astrologers to get
round this difficulty by going over to the sidereal zodiac,
that is, calculating a horoscope by reference to the actual
constellations in the sky. This may be scientifically valid,
but it destroys part of the beauty of the traditional association between the signs and the changing seasons of the
year. Leo, for example, lies traditionally in August and is
ruled by the Sun which is generally at its fullest glory in
that month. Leonian types have a summer-like character;
they are warm, friendly, and joyful. Capricorn, by contrast, lying in January, has the hard, cold, stony character
appropriate to a winter sign, and Capricornian types show
these qualities. This connection between signs and months
has the appeal of a powerful and beautiful myth. To allow
for the precession of the equinoxes is to destroy this completely.

Another thing that is scientifically unjustifiable is the
theory of rulerships. In what sense can it be proved that
Mars 'rules' Aries, or that Venus 'rules' Taurus? Here
again we have an idea which has a symbolic and mytho-

logical value, but which makes nonsense to the scientist. The same is true of the planetary aspects. A square be-tween two planets on the astrologer's chart bears no re-lation to the true interaction of planetary forces in the solar system – or if it does it is such a gross oversimplifica-tion as to be meaningless. How, the scientist asks, can the infinitely subtle interplay of planetary fields be reduced to five or six clear-cut 'angles'?

These objections are obvious, but to admit them is not to admit that traditional astrology has no value. As I have said it has a symbolic value. Let me try to explain more precisely what I mean by this.

A symbol is something that strikes a chord within the mind of the person who is seeing it. Certain symbols are the result of conditioning – traffic lights for example or the shaking of hands. Others have been with the human race for so long that they have become instinctive. I would put the astrological symbols in this second category. The ideas represented by the astrological terms are ideals that lie very deep in the human mind – as deep as the urge to love and the instinct for self-preservation.

Astrology is a symbolic way of stating a belief that the inner universe within each man is a reflection of the outer universe with its stars and planets. No other science or system of divination expresses this relationship between outer and inner as elegantly and as satisfyingly as astrology.

If the astrological symbols are truly a reflection of man's inner forces, then to understand and manipulate the sym-bols is to understand and manipulate those forces. The occultists of ancient and medieval times had various ways of attempting to control these forces. The alchemist linked them with the seven basic metals which were, of course, governed by the seven traditional planets. The main pur-pose of the alchemist was not to make gold. This was only an outward aid to an inner purpose, which was to trans-form the dross of his own base nature into the gold of spirit. These inner forces were also recognised by the

Jewish cabalist who identified them with the ten Sephiroth of the Tree of Life, the ten great channels of divine power. The astrologer connected them with the heavenly bodies. In each case the purpose was the same: to bring the inner forces under control.

The early Christian theologian Thomas Aquinas put this very well. He said that the stars govern our basic natures. Most people never rise above their basic natures and so most people are ruled by the stars – that is to say, symbolically speaking, they are unable to control their own inner forces. But, says Aquinas, there are certain human beings who are able to cultivate a higher nature which is not subservient to the stars. These people have true free will.

So here you have a powerful set of symbols relating to forces in the psyche. And what you see when you look at a horoscope is how these forces are balanced within the individuals – which are likely to work in his favour and which are likely to work against him.

The Hindus have an interesting theory about the horoscope, which ties in with their theories on reincarnation. To them an individual's horoscope is a kind of balance sheet of assets and liabilities carried over from his previous existence. Whether one believes in this or not it is possible to take a very positive view of the bad factors in one's chart, regarding them as a challenge to one's resources.

People often resent the idea of a human being starting off with advantages or disadvantages written in his stars. They say that it diminishes freedom of will and therefore diminishes the moral responsibility for his actions. But to my mind this is a senseless objection. No one denies the fact that certain people are born taller, more intelligent, or keener-sighted than others. But no one believes that this calls freedom of will in question. Everyone's freedom is limited in certain areas and not limited in others, and if a person tries to convince himself that he is free in all respects he will, in fact, cease to be free at all because his delusion will enslave him. Only by recognising the existence of the unfree areas of life can one be truly free in the free areas. And this is where astrology could help. A proper understanding of the cosmic pattern under which one was born could point the way of attainment of freedom.

Let me anticipate an objection to what I have been saying. It might go like this. 'Your ideas about symbolism are all very well, but if your system is purely symbolic and has no basis in fact then why do you need to know the exact time and place of birth when you are casting a horoscope?' This is a tricky question, and it is impossible to answer it in scientific terms. I look upon all systems of divination as games with different sets of rules. Obeying the rules enables a person to get 'switched on', to lift himself into a different mental state where he is able to see things about people and events that he would not normally be able to see. It does not much matter what the rules are as long as you obey them consistently. Instead of the astrologer choosing the time and place of birth he could just as well choose the time and place where the child's first tooth was observed or some other equally arbitrarily chosen event; the point is that if he obeys his own rules consistently the system will still work.

This ability to get 'switched on' to a state where predictions can be made does not, of course, occur in everyone, and certain people have it to a greater degree than others. Another thing about this ability is that it is affected by the strength of a person's belief in the system of divination he is using – his faith in it, if you like. Now the effectiveness of astrology has been greatly helped by the fact that belief in it has been strengthened by its apparent scientific basis. But, as I have shown, traditional astrology will not stand this test of scientific analysis. It is therefore time that astrologers faced up to the choice that is before them: either they can continue to practise the old traditional astrology with its profound and beautiful system of symbolism, in which case they must realise that their system can never be proved except by results; or they can take the scientific path, in which case they will have to jettison most of the old theories and start again from scratch, building on strict scientific principles.

As I have said, I believe that the scientific approach will ultimately prevail; but this is not to say that the old astrological tradition need be relegated to the status of a museum piece. Alchemy was superseded by chemistry in the same way, but today there is more interest than ever in alchemy, whose wonderful subtle symbolism is an inspiration to many people in search of hidden truths. Alchemy has, in a sense, raised itself to a higher, spiritual function, leaving chemistry to deal with the more prosaic business of transmuting matters.

In the same way astrology will, I believe, take on a different purpose, while a new astrology will be born from the womb of science.

Appendix 1

Anecdotes from the Astrological Scrapbook

MANY thousands of predictions have been made by astrologers since Babylonian times. Some of these have come true, some have not. Here is a selection of some of the more interesting ones, successful and unsuccessful, as well as some other curious incidents involving astrology.

Saved by a Prophecy

The Roman emperor, Tiberius, suppressed astrology because he believed that predictions might be dangerous to him. At the same time he secretly consulted astrologers for his own purposes. Often, after one of these secret consultations, he would have the astrologer thrown into the sea from his cliff-hanging palace on Capri to prevent the wretch from leaking out any information that might undermine the emperor's position. An astrologer named Thrasyllus was summoned to the Royal Palace, and after the consultation Tiberius asked if the astrologer ever read his own stars and if so what they indicated for his future. Thrasyllus examined the positions of the stars and as he did so became agitated. 'Your majesty,' he said, 'my calculations tell me that I am very near to death.' Tiberius, impressed by the astrologer's skill, explained that he had intended to kill him, but had now changed his mind. Thereafter Thrasyllus became an intimate and honoured friend of the emperor.

A Last-minute Fulfilment

While the Roman emperor Caracalla was waging war in Mesopotamia he sent orders back to his regent in Rome, Maternianus, to hold a meeting with astrologers to find out if there was any plot against the emperor's life. This was done, and the astrologers concluded that Caracalla's colonel, Macrinus, was planning to kill him. Maternianus, who hated Macrinus, gleefully sent a letter off to the emperor, telling him the news. But the letter had unexpected consequences. When it arrived Caracalla was engaged in sport and ordered Macrinus to open it. Until that moment Macrinus had no intention of harming the emperor, but when he read the contents of the letter he saw that his only course was to kill Caracalla and ordered his servant to do this.

A Cunning Astrologer

The medieval king, Louis XI of France, was told that an astrologer had predicted the death of a woman of whom the king was very fond. He summoned the prophet and, after expressing his displeasure, asked him: 'You, who know everything, when will you die?' The astrologer, suspecting the king's intentions, replied: 'Sire, three days before your majesty.' Fear and superstition overcame the king's anger, and thereafter he took particular care of the clever astrologer.

An Anti-climax

The year 1186 was thought by astrologers to be a particularly fateful one because of an impending conjunction of planets in the sign of Libra. Because of the 'airy' nature of Libra it was thought that the world would be afflicted by terrible wind storms. In some countries people went so far as to build special underground shelters to escape the storms. As it happened, nothing of the kind occurred, though some astrologers claimed that part of the adverse prediction had been fulfilled by Saladin's victories in the Holy Land the following year.

A Victory Predicted

In June 1386, during a war between the two Italian houses of Carrara and Della Scala, the astrologer Blasius of Parma predicted that if the Carrara army engaged in battle on a particular day they would win and take their opponents prisoner. At first the battle went the other way and the Carrara troops were pursued to the town wall, whereupon a bystander derided Blasius for his prediction. He replied calmly: 'Either it will come out as I have said or the heavens will fall.' Sure enough, the unrouted portion of the Carrara army took the pursuers in the rear. Caught between two forces, the Della Scala troops were taken prisoner, and Blasius's prediction was fulfilled.

A Papal Death

In the year 1472, an astrologer called Perre le Lorrain predicted the death of Pope Paul II because of a comet which had appeared. This incurred the anger of the pope, and the astrologer was put in prison and told that he would be executed if his prediction proved false. On the afternoon of the day in question His Holiness was still in good health and Lorrain's friends visited him in prison expecting that he would soon be put to death. He confidently told them to await the hour, and sure enough the pope died before the end of the day. Lorrain was then released and honoured.

Royal Seer

One of the most prolific prophets of all time was the 16th-century French astrologer and occultist, Nostradamas, who was employed at the court of Catherine de Medicis. In a series of quatrains he made a number of startling predictions, one of which was as follows:

> The young lion shall overcome the old
> In war-like field in single fight
> In a golden cage he will pierce the eye
> Two wounds one, then die a cruel death.

This was interpreted as foretelling the death of Catherine's husband, Henry II. On July 1, 1559, the king competed in a joust with the young Comte de Montgommeri. The count's lance pierced the king's visor, and a splinter wounded him above the right eye. After ten days of agony the king died. The word 'lion' in the verse referred to the fact that both contestants wore a lion emblem. The 'cage of gold' was the king's gilt visor.

Nostradamus also foresaw a number of events much farther ahead, such as the French Revolution, which he described in a number of quatrains. He called it *le Commun Advenement* (the advent of the Commons). One of the events of the Revolution which he described was the attempted escape of Louis XIV and Marie Antoinette, which ended with their capture at Varennes. Nostradamus had written in a quatrain that:

> At night will come through the Forest of Reines,
> A married couple, by devious route,
> Herne, the white stone, the monk in grey, into Varennes,
> The elected Capet – the result will be tempest, fire.
> > blood – and cutting off.

Other quatrains are thought to foretell the Second World War. In them he mentions a character called

'Hister' which had been interpreted as a code name for Hitler.

An Astronomer dabbles in Astrology

The Danish astronomer Tycho Brahe was, along with Kepler, Copernicus, and Galileo, one of the founders of modern astronomy. He also practised astrology and was official astrologer to the emperor Rudolph II of Austria. In 1563, at the age of seventeen, Brahe predicted that in the year 1665 a plague would sweep Europe. The prophecy was fulfilled in the form of the Great Plague which lasted from 1665 to 1666. In 1572 Brahe observed the appearance of a new star in Cassiopeia which, he said, heralded the birth of a prince who would wage war against Germany, but would disappear in 1632. This description fitted Gustavus Adolphus of Sweden who swept through most of Central Europe, but was killed at the battle of Lutzen in 1632.

Bad Omens for a Marriage

Ebenezer Sibly, one of the few astrologers of any note in the sceptical 18th century, describes in his book *The Science of Astrology* how he was approached by a lady seeking advice on whether she should marry. Sibly compared the horoscopes of the lady and her prospective husband and found that all the signs were against the success of the marriage. 'I could not find a single configuration in the one that bore the least harmony or similitude with the other. The benefic stars in the angles of one figure were opposed to the malefics in the angles of the other. The *masculine* temperature was strongest in the female horoscope ... while in the man's geniture, the effeminacy of the *female* influence was but too apparent.'

Sibly counselled against the marriage, but evidently the lady was attracted by the prospect of financial gain, and insisted on going ahead. As predicted, the marriage was a disaster: 'The new-married pair were put to bed – *where love and joy should take their fill*: but such was the singularity of the case, that the bride rose up with the sun, and, having been refused that participation of fortune her friends had blazoned out, and finding no other allurement to supply that defect, she immediately deserted her husband, who never took the pains to retrieve her; and she has since attached herself to two other persons, by both of whom she has had children.'

A Plot on Hitler's Life

On 2 November 1939, the Swiss astrologer Karl Ernst Krafft sent a letter to the German security service predicting that Hitler's life would be in danger between 7th and 10th November, and mentioning the 'possibility of an attempt at assassination by the use of explosive material'. On the evening of 8 November Hitler attended a celebration at the Bürgerbrau Keller in Munich. He left earlier than expected to return to Berlin, and a few minutes after his departure a bomb hidden in a pillar exploded killing seven people and wounding sixty-three others.

Wishful Thinking

A less accurate prediction concerning Hitler was recorded by the English astrologer R. H. Naylor in his *Year Book for 1933*. 'Hitler,' he wrote, 'is a son of the elusive planet Neptune. He looks to Mussolini as his example. Whereas Mussolini will go from strength to strength, Hitler will go from weakness to weakness. Finally he and his party will run into a mass of schemes and complications which will eclipse them.' If only Naylor's prediction had been right!

Fixing Independence Day

When Burma was due to receive independent status the day first decided on by the British was 6 January 1948. The Burmese, however, insisted on changing it to 4 January, the Sunday after the Moon's third quarter. This was considered more auspicious by the astrologers.

Appendix 2
Glossary of Terms

Affliction   A planet is said to be 'afflicted' when it is badly placed in relation to one or more other planets, for example if it is in square aspect to another.

Angles   See page 54.

Apogee   The point in a planet's orbit where it is farthest from the earth.

Ascendant   The part of the zodiac at the eastern horizon at the time of birth.

Aspects   The angles formed between planets in a horoscope. See page 58.

Benefics   The planets which, in traditional astrology, were thought to exercise a good influence, namely Sun, Moon, Jupiter, and Venus.

Cadent   See page 54.

Caput Draconis and Cauda Draconis   The Dragon's Head and Tail. See Nodes of the Moon.

Cardinal signs   See page 27.

Climacteric   A Climacteric is a critical year in an individual's life. Every 7th and 9th year of a life is a climacteric because the Moon repeats its squares and trines every 7 and 9 years respectively. The 7th, 14th, 21st, 28th, and so on, are unfortunate; whereas the 9th, 18th, 27th, 36th etc are fortunate. The Grand Climacteric is the 63rd year, when good and evil forces coincide. If the Moon is well placed at birth then the person's life continues after the Grand Climacteric; otherwise life comes to an end.

Conjunction   One of the aspects. See page 58.

Cusp   The dividing line between one house and another.

Decan   One third of a sign, or ten degrees. The signs are subdivided in this way, each decan having a different quality. The system is especially common in India.

Decumbiture   A horoscope cast for a sick person to see whether or not he will recover.

Detriment   See 'rulerships'.

Dignity   See 'exaltations'.

Dominant   A planet which is placed near to one of the angles or in some other way that gives it a special importance.

Ecliptic   The Sun's apparent path around the earth. See page 11.

Elections   Times chosen by astrologers as being auspicious for the initiation of some enterprise.

Elements   Fire, Earth, Air and Water. See page 27.

Ephemeris   A set of tables giving planetary positions for a particular year, used by astrologers in making the calculations for a horoscope.

Equinoxes   The points at which the ecliptic crosses the equator.

Exaltations   Each planet has a sign in which it is said to be 'exalted', meaning that its influence will be strong and favourable. The opposite sign is referred to as the planet's 'fall', and denotes weakness. The exaltations are as follows:

Sun		
	is exalted in	
		Aries
Moon		
	„	Taurus
Mercury		
	„	Virgo
Venus		
	„	Pisces
Mars		
	„	Capricorn
Jupiter		
	„	Cancer
Saturn		
	„	Libra

There is no agreement among astrologers as to the exaltations of the three 'new' planets. In the older terminology the word 'dignified' was used instead of exalted.

Fixed signs   See page 27.

Fixed Stars   An old term referring to the stars as opposed to the planets.

Friendly planets   Certain planets are 'friendly' to one another, others are 'inimical'. For example, Venus and Mars are inimical because they rule, respectively, Taurus and Scorpio, which are opposed to one another in the zodiac. By contrast, Venus and the Moon are friendly because the Moon rules Cancer, which is a water sign, and the element water complements the earth element of Taurus.

Horary Astrology   The branch of astrology involving the casting of horoscopes for a particular time in order to answer questions about an event or enterprise – as opposed to natal astrology which gives general answers based on the birth horoscope. See page 69.

Horoscope   Chart of the heavens at the time of birth.

Imum Coeli   The 'lowest heaven' i.e. the cusp of the 4th house, which lies opposite to the *medium coeli* or 'mid-heaven'. Usually written as IC.

Inferior Conjunction   The conjunction of a planet with the Sun when the planet is between the Sun and the Earth.

Lights   A term used to refer to the Sun and Moon. It has crept into everyday use in such expressions as 'he acted according to his lights'. The lights are also sometimes called 'luminaries'.

Malefics   Planets considered in traditional astrology to be of evil influence. These were Saturn and Mars. Some modern astrologers have added Uranus and Neptune.

Medium Coeli   The mid-heaven, i.e. the part of the zodiac immediately overhead at the time of birth. It is usually abbreviated to MC.

Meridian   A line running north and south and passing through the mid-heaven.

Mundane   Pertaining to the houses, as opposed to the signs of the zodiac.

Mutable signs   See page 27.

Native   The subject of a horoscope.

Nodes   The points at which the orbit of a planet crosses the ecliptic. In certain systems of astrology, particularly in India, the nodes of the Moon are considered to be of great importance in a horoscope. The Moon's ascending node (i.e. the point where the Moon's path on its upward journey crosses the ecliptic) is known as the Dragon's Head and is thought to be auspicious. The descending node is known as the Dragon's Tail and is considered malefic.

Opposition   One of the aspects. See page 59.

Orb   The margin within which a planetary aspect is effective, usually 7 or 8 degrees.

Pars Fortunae   The 'Part of Fortune', an imaginary point in the horoscope, found by determining the distance of the Moon from the ascendant and then subtracting the longitude of the Sun. *The Pars Fortunae* was once thought to be of great importance, but is used much less by astrologers today.

Perigree   The opposite of apogee, i.e. the point in a planet's orbit where it is closest to the earth.

Precession   Literally a 'moving backwards'. The equinoxes move back through the zodiac at the rate of about one sign every 2,000 years. See page 13.

Radical   This word refers to the characteristics of the birth horoscope as opposed to those in the progressed horoscope (see page 63) or to the positions of the transiting planets.

Rectification   If a native's exact time of birth is not known or is doubtful, it can be 'rectified' by working backwards from significant events in his life and deducing where the planets would have been at birth in order to bring about the events in question.

Retrograde   A planet is said to be retrograde when it appears to move backwards through the zodiac. This is an illusion caused by the relation between the speed of a planet and the speed of the earth's movement.

Rulerships   Each sign is 'ruled' by a planet. The influence of a planet is particularly strong if it is placed in the sign over which it rules. The opposite sign in the zodiac to the one which it rules is known as its 'detriment'. If a planet is in detriment its influence is weak.

Sextie An aspect. See page 59.

Sidereal Pertaining to, or measured from, the stars. From the Latin *sidus*, a star.

Solstices The two points where the ecliptic is farthest from the equator. See page 12.

Square An aspect. See page 59.

Succedent See page 54.

Superior Conjunction The conjunction of a planet with the Sun when the planet is on the far side of the Sun from the Earth.

Transits A transit occurs when a planet passes over an important or sensitive position in the birth chart. To 'consult one's transits' for a particular day means to ascertain where the planets will be on that day and then see if they form any important aspects with the planets in one's birth chart.

Trine An aspect. See page 59.

ABOUT THE AUTHOR

Christopher McIntosh was born in 1943 and educated at Edinburgh Academy and Christ Church, Oxford. While an undergraduate he became drawn to the study of occultism, comparative religion, and related subjects. His first book, *The Astrologers and their Creed*, was published in 1969. Since leaving university he has worked in the field of publishing and journalism, and is at present on the editorial staff of *Country Life*, to which he has contributed articles on architecture, topography, and folklore. He lives in Hertfordshire with his wife and two sons.

ACKNOWLEDGEMENTS

We are grateful to the following for the illustrations, and for permission to use copyright prints and photographs:

Oxford Illustrators Ltd; Fox Photos, 6; Mansell Collection, 7, 8; Metropolitan Photo Service Inc, 9; Radio Times Hulton Picture Library, 1, 2a, 5, Ronan Picture Library, 2b, 3; John Webb, 4a, 4b. The quotation from the musical, *Hair*, is reproduced by permission of United Artists Music Ltd. The following publishers are acknowledged for other quotations in the text: L. N. Fowler & Co, Penguin Books, The Theosophical Publishing House, and the Ninth House Publishing Co.